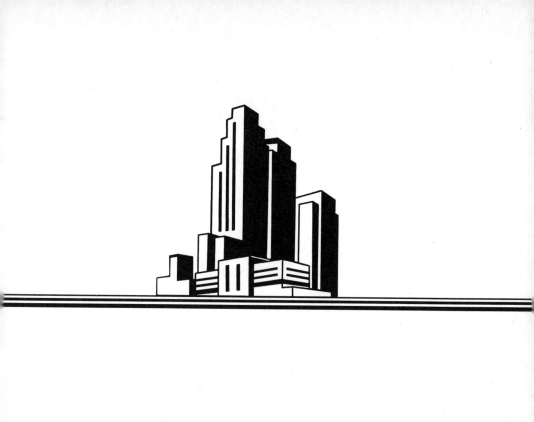

URBAN NATION

WHY WE NEED TO GIVE POWER BACK TO THE CITIES TO MAKE CANADA STRONG

ALAN BROADBENT

HarperCollins*PublishersLtd*

Urban Nation
© 2008 by Alan Broadbent. All rights reserved.

Published by HarperCollins Publishers Ltd.

First edition

HarperCollins books may be purchased for educational, business, or sales promotional use through our Special Markets Department.

HarperCollins Publishers Ltd
2 Bloor Street East, 20th Floor
Toronto, Ontario, Canada
M4W 1A8

www.harpercollins.ca

Library and Archives Canada Cataloguing in Publication

Broadbent, Alan
Urban nation : why we need to give power back to the cities to make Canada strong / Alan Broadbent.

ISBN 978-0-00-200883-9

1. Municipal government—Canada.
2. Urban policy—Canada.
3. Urbanization—Canada.
4. Canada—Emigration and immigration.
5. Federal-local relations—Canada.
6. Provincial-local relations—Canada.
I. Title.

JS1710.b76 2008   320.8'50971   C2008-900838-3

HC 9 8 7 6 5 4 3 2 1

Printed and bound in the United States
Text design by Sharon Kish

CONTENTS

For Louie, Sam, and Matt

Introduction

WITH GLOWING HEARTS
Canada's Invisible Cities

It started on March 3, 1993, at Toronto's Sheraton Centre hotel across from City Hall, where a large and eager crowd gathered to hear a visionary immigrant challenge a member of the Canadian establishment on whether Toronto should declare its independence from Canada's Confederation and go it on its own. Or, at the very least, negotiate a new arrangement with the country. A lot of them had already made up their minds, and they were restless and ready to be inspired. Would they take to the streets, refuse to pay their taxes, or mount a mighty resistance to the unfairness they all sensed?

This could have been a scene from another age. It might have been John Alexander Macdonald from Glasgow, or William Lyon Mackenzie and his followers who surged up Yonge Street and mounted the 1837 rebellion against the "Family Compact," or the anti-amalgamation crowd behind rebel former mayor John Sewell and Citizens for Local Democracy, the cyber-labelled C4LD, 160 years later.

In fact, it was something more sedate, but which had reverberations that began to change the conversation in Canada towards the plight of the big cities, a conversation that was picked up by a future prime minister, and one that fuelled municipal unrest into the start of the twenty-first century.

The visionary was Joe Berridge, a normally affable and well-mannered man occasionally given to provocative and inspiring commentary on the urban condition. Berridge was a well-known urban planner, a transplanted Welshman from up the ancient valleys who had worked as a Toronto city planner before forming his own firm, Urban Strategies, and who was on his way to becoming one of the top international planners working around the world. The prince of the establishment was now-Senator David Smith, a Toronto lawyer who had been a federal member of Parliament and a cabinet minister, and was one of the big movers and shakers in the Liberal Party of Canada. Smith represented Canada As We Know It, and Berridge was the challenger.

The occasion was a debate the Canadian Urban Institute staged on the topic, "Should the Greater Toronto Area form a separate province within Canada?"—a play on the ongoing Canadian obsession with Quebec separation. Berridge argued for the motion, Smith against.

Berridge, in his compelling style, put the challenge dramatically: Here's the deal, Canada; give us our freedom, and we'll send you the money we send now through the federal wealth-sharing programs, indexed to inflation, forever. You only want Toronto for our money, he said. We'll thrive unleashed from the strictures of federal and provincial governments, because we'll be able to construct policies and programs in a nimble way that will let us respond to international competitive challenges. His argument was based on the notion that the Toronto region was a dynamic economic producer of wealth, and that it contributed far more to the national coffers than it received back in tax-paid goods and services. These were the funds that were transferred to the less wealthy parts of the country through equalization payments and other grants, and which funded the large bureaucracies of those governments. But Toronto had to go to the federal and provincial governments to plead for the infrastructure that would fuel its economic growth, things like an improved airport, roads, rail service, and financial industry regulatory liberalization.

Smith replied that Canada was a great success, that we had a tried and true way of dealing with these things, that the constitutional mechanisms for change were complicated and arduous, that the federal and provincial governments would surely find ways to deal with local discontent, and that he was frankly a little surprised that the good people of Toronto did not recognize, and indeed were not more grateful for, all the things that the government did for them.

Berridge won the debate handily, as the audience divided over 90 percent for him. It was a room full of urban wonks, people who worked in municipal, provincial, and federal government departments, academics, politicians, and business people whose main markets were governments and their agencies. It was the first time I had heard Berridge's argument put that strongly and in quite that way, and it fascinated me.

What if Toronto decided it wanted to separate from Canada? What if it took a page from Quebec's playbook and began to mount a separatist movement? What would be the response of the rest of the country to its claims of historic grievances, and to its grossly unfair treatment?

What might its grievances be? It is underrepresented in the House of Commons, with fewer seats than its population would warrant, and so doesn't enjoy representation by population. It annually sends much more money to Ottawa than it gets back in goods and services from the government. It has a citizenry that is distinctly different from the country as a whole, made up of close to 50 percent immigrants and 50 percent visible minorities. It is focused on the challenges of the new economy in the midst of a country still focused on the old economy. It consistently gets ignored as federal government support puts comedy museums in Montreal and infectious disease centres in Winnipeg. It gets less money per capita for social programs than other parts of the country. It is tired of being the cash cow of Confederation.

In many ways, Toronto has a better argument for distinct treatment than does Quebec, or even the Alberta "firewall" secessionists. Unlike Quebec, which is "bought off" year after year with more powers, more money, and more attention, or Alberta, for which Canada blackens its eye in the international environmental community by ignoring the massive pollution and contamination of its water resources so that the province can enrich itself on oil sands dollars, Toronto is expected to be the quiet donor to the federal coffers, enduring decade after decade of empty promises from federal leaders who only show up to speak at one of the huge fundraising dinners that keep their party machinery running.

Toronto's role in Confederation, it seems, is to keep quiet and send money.

But the denizens of Canada's largest urban region are restless. And they are not alone. In Vancouver there is also a sense of unrest, as people are beginning to see that city occupying the same place in the context of British Columbia as Toronto does nationally. And even in Montreal, people are beginning to wonder why the golden goose of Quebec is propping up the rest of the province.

This is a story of Canadian cities coming of age, of having become over the last fifty years the dominant political entity in the country, and now realizing the inadequacy of the tools at hand to control their own destinies. The story plays out in city halls across the country as mayors and councils try to stretch municipal budgets to meet growing demands for goods and services while federal and provincial coffers overflow. The discontent that first erupted in Toronto has spread to other cities across the country as their leaders recognize the basic disconnection between the vast potential of our urban regions and the constraints our government structures put in the way. And it will play out in provincial legislatures and on Parliament Hill in Ottawa, as first ministers slowly realize that fealty to old constitutional structures is a precious conceit in a world where competing urban regions will blaze the arc of history.

Why Cities?

My interest in the topic of cities developed slowly. During the 1960s, when I was at the University of British Columbia, I read Jane Jacobs' *Death and Life of the Great American Cities* (1961), which began to form in my awareness the city as a dynamic interplay of forces. And Jacobs' 1984 book, *Cities and the Wealth of Nations*, really put cities in the forefront of my mind.

In Toronto in the 1970s, a large number of my friends were working as planners, and eventually as senior civil servants, in the municipal government. It was a dynamic time in the city of Toronto, during which a group of activist councillors that included future mayor John Sewell, William Kilbourn, and Colin Vaughan encouraged Mayor David Crombie to embrace an agenda that included the building of housing and the retention and strengthening of neighbourhoods. Where other cities, particularly in the United States, were demolishing downtown neighbourhoods for expressways, office towers, and large-scale housing projects, Toronto was able to retain strong downtown neighbourhoods and manage growth in a way that genuflected to the mixed-use ideas of Jane Jacobs. Crombie spearheaded the building of the St. Lawrence housing development in the lower east quadrant of downtown, a landmark development that garnered fame for including seamlessly a range of income levels in a high-density project that didn't look massive, and which included parks and recreational amenities, all within a ten-minute walk of downtown. To watch all this happen, and so much more in that era, was a revelation as to what was possible, and an endorsement of the city's high capacity to achieve notable things, when there was money and friendly governments on Parliament Hill in Ottawa and Queen's Park in Toronto.

I was working in business, in the process of forming a private investment company, when at the end of the 1980s a friend suggested I get involved with some people starting the Canadian Urban Institute (CUI), so I joined the founding board and helped build the Institute. This brought me more closely in contact with city issues, not just in Toronto but across the country. It also brought me into contact with Jane Jacobs, whom I had known only as a reader of her books. It also gave me the opportunity to moderate the Berridge-Smith debate.

Ideas That Matter

In 1995, my colleagues and I began to plan a celebration of Jane Jacobs' work. I felt that Jane's important body of work was not as well known as it should be, particularly among progressive people in the US who were dealing with issues and problems that would have been helped had they known of her thinking. And I thought we needed to inject the question of the place of cities in Canada into the public discourse, as a way of elevating their importance in the public consciousness and among the political elite.

Working with my colleague Mary Rowe, we organized a five-day series of events in October 1997 that looked at the whole range of Jacobs' work, on streets, neighbourhoods, and cities, on economies, on ethics, and on nature. We called it Jane Jacobs: Ideas That Matter. We later took the phrase Ideas That Matter for the name of the organization that would be centred on Jane's ideas, but which would also look for other innovative ideas that highlighted the interconnectedness of things, which had become Jane's compelling observation at the end of her life. There were the usual panel discussions and speeches, there were performances by singers and artists, there were tours, and there was even a canoe trip down the Humber River led by Joe Berridge. The celebration took place all over the city, with people getting from place to place via Toronto's "red rocket" streetcars. It culminated in a big meal served in the foyer of BCE Place in downtown Toronto, under the soaring canopy designed by Santiago Calatrava—Jane's idea of commensality, or sharing together.

A Charter for Cities in Canada

In the spring of 1999, my colleagues and I convened a group of people to look into the place of cities in Canada, at a small invitational conference we called The Evolution of Toronto. This was a direct response to some of the interest, and urgings to continue, which had come up at Ideas That Matter. We commissioned a few papers on issues like environment, finance, and government in the city, and held a two-day meeting at the Royal Alexandra Theatre in Toronto, which David Mirvish donated for the purpose. (The meeting subsequently became referred to as The Mirvish Meeting.) We published a book of the proceedings of that meeting, called Toronto: *Considering Self-Government*, which garnered enough interest that it went to a second printing.

At the end of the meeting, we issued an invitation to those who wanted to continue these discussions to gather in my boardroom. About twenty-five people showed up, including Jane Jacobs, three former Toronto mayors (Crombie, Sewell, and Barbara Hall), journalists Richard Gwyn, Michael Valpy, and Colin Vaughan, University of Toronto urban academics Patricia McCarney, Meric Gertler, and

Carl Amrhein, and people who had been around these issues for years in government, such as former Ontario deputy minister Don Stevenson, former Toronto alderman Richard Gilbert, and municipal finance expert Enid Slack. This group met every few months for well over a year.

There was remarkable consensus on what the problems were, and a fairly quick identification of the need to broaden the awareness of them. After a few meetings, the idea of a charter document arose, much like the ones on cities adopted by the European Union and the Federation of Canadian Municipalities. We produced *Towards a Greater Toronto Charter*, a statement of some basic principles of authority and accountability for the city region, as well as a description of some of the powers we thought the Toronto region should have. It was not very difficult to come up with these powers; they are roughly those of a province, in the Canadian context. Following publication, the document was endorsed by a number of local municipal governments. While those endorsements didn't effectively mean much, they indicated that there is much more that unites people and governments across the Toronto region than divides them. And they indicated a strong sense among elected municipal officials that they lacked the powers and respect they needed to be able to fulfill their responsibilities to citizens.

The group that had developed the Charter continued to meet, turning their efforts to strategies and tactics that might result in some change in practice between the three levels of government. The meetings were recorded for the CBC Radio program *Ideas*.

I had always thought that, ultimately, this would not be a problem to be solved with logic or a better argument; rather, there would have to be some political energy and action. As Conference Board of Canada president Anne Golden, who had done a milestone report on the future of the Toronto region in 1995, put it, "It's not as if we haven't put the right argument to the right people in the right place at the right time before." This view had been bolstered in a discussion Jane had had with people from the Privy Council Office in Ottawa, who asked what the Canadian mayors were saying collectively.

The C5 Mayors

We had encountered the collective voice of Canadian mayors and cities, the Federation of Canadian Municipalities. A membership organization, the FCM represents over 1,600 municipalities, ranging from Toronto, at 2.5 million people (city proper, not the region), to Tugaske, Saskatchewan, at 116 people. The FCM's Big City Caucus has twenty-two members, but over half of these have populations of less than half a million people, hardly an international description of a big city. One of the great challenges facing the FCM is to arrive at consensus across the 1,600 members, or even across the twenty-two in the Big City Caucus. As such, it did not have a reputation as a powerhouse politically, although it had done excellent work in cooperation among towns, villages, and cities, and in gaining some favourable tax treatment for municipalities. But clearly the PCO officials had not heard from FCM, and suggested that an effort to rouse a new political voice from the mayors of the large cities might bear fruit.

We had talked about mobilizing mayors before, but were a little uncertain how to go about it. In 1998, Toronto had been forcefully amalgamated by the province, over the objections of the constituent cities and most citizens. The cities that had made up Metropolitan Toronto, with their distinct city councils, had been made one city with a large new council, and former North York mayor Mel Lastman had been elected mayor. Lastman was a character, given to periodic showmanship and mugging and making deals with big developers. He had little time or inclination for cooperating with other cities, and his relationships with other levels of government were famously variable, ranging from smiling photo ops to colourful harangues. On the other hand, Canada's two other urban regions, Vancouver and Montreal, had good and steady mayors. Philip Owen in Vancouver had been elected to three terms, was the son of highly regarded British Columbia lieutenant governor Walter Owen, and had guided Vancouver with a steady hand. Pierre Bourque in Montreal was the former head of the Montreal Botanical Garden, and had been mayor since 1994. Al Duerr was mayor of Calgary, having won four terms of office, and was both popular with his constituents and very bright.

But the most noteworthy mayor in Canada in late 2000 was Glen Murray, elected mayor of Winnipeg in 1998 after running as an openly gay candidate. A former city councillor, Murray was tremendously articulate and an avid devotee of Jane Jacobs' ideas. Jane phoned Murray to see what he thought about getting some of the big-city mayors together to push for more control of destiny for Canada's cities, and he responded enthusiastically, offering to help recruit the others. We had originally thought of four cities, the three urban regions and Calgary, because of its oil-based economic clout. Winnipeg is Canada's eighth-largest city, with Edmonton, Ottawa, and Quebec City lying between it and the four mentioned above, but thanks to Murray's excitement for the idea, Winnipeg was in.

We held the first meeting of what we termed the C5 Mayors in Winnipeg in May of 2001. Each delegation was headed by its mayor, but also included leaders of business (the board of trade or chamber of commerce), social sector (United Way, Centraide, or Community Foundation), and labour (either the local labour council or a prominent labour leader). Some of the mayors brought along additional participants, like the chief administrative officer or city manager, a prominent local businessperson, or a trusted adviser like Ivan Head, who accompanied Mayor Owen. The agenda began with a talk from Jane Jacobs about the purpose of meeting and the problem with the status of cities in Canada. Then each city made a presentation, much of which focused on itsfiscal plight compared to its needs. The next day, after an intense morning meeting, the mayors met with an initially skeptical press, who seemed to think they were grandstanding. That, of course, was part of the point of the meeting, and they managed to get some good coverage the next day.

That first meeting set the pattern for those that followed. Most particularly, there was strong participation by the non-mayoral delegates. Many of them had not thought about the problem of the way cities were treated, and when it dawned on them how debilitating it was, and how many of the issues they were dealing with could be traced to this structural defect, they became very interested, and some became rather intense. That cohort of people grew more passionate, and we termed them the C5 Civil Society, or C5 Civil.

The C5 Mayors and C5 Civil met two more times, in Vancouver in January of 2002 and in Montreal in June 2002 at the time of newly elected mayor Gerald Tremblay's Montreal Summit. The C5 Civil met two more times without their mayors, in Toronto in January and again in October 2003. In late 2003, Toronto elected David Miller as mayor, and he immediately embraced the issue vocally and publicly. I had always thought the mayors themselves should be the driving force behind a national voice for cities, and with Miller leading from Toronto, the C5 could fade into history.

The C5 had a short life span, but it served as one of a number of agents in putting the issues into both the political and public discourse. Others were various boards of trade, especially in Toronto and Calgary, the Toronto United Way and the Conference Board of Canada under Anne Golden, the Winnipeg branch of the Canadian Union of Public

Employees under Paul Moist, the Canada West Foundation under Roger Gibbins, the TD Bank through the work of Don Drummond and Derek Burleton, and latterly the Toronto City Summit Alliance under chair David Pecaut.

Focus on Finance

The work of Ideas That Matter stayed "on the file," but with less active convening. Jane Jacobs was busy writing what would be her last book, *Dark Age Ahead*, and when Jane was writing she did not want to make time for activism, or at least not sustained activism. Mary Rowe and I had a conversation about where the gaps were, because so much activity was now underway in 2004 and 2005, and we both agreed that the big one was fiscal. There was a lot of misinformation or fuzzy thinking afoot. For example, when politicians talked about channelling more money to cities, about hotel taxes or shares of gas tax, they tended to do so in terms of a panacea. In fact, compared to municipal budget deficits, such taxes generate funds that are barely material. The big tax instruments, the ones that provide the large revenues that can make a real difference, are income and sales taxes. We felt there was a need for an organization to provide such ongoing commentary.

And we knew who should head it: Enid Slack, the "go-to" person on municipal finance in Canada. Enid had been mentored by Richard Bird and Harry Kitchen, the previous generation's go-to guys, and had been part of all our activities since Toronto Charter days. So, together with Enid, we approached Janice Stein at the Munk Centre at the University of Toronto and set up the Institute for Municipal Finance and Governance (IMFG), which has since become a focal point for research on those topics, for teaching students, and for convening conversations about the future of cities in Canada.

From Hinterland to City Streets

Canada is bound in a structure of government designed by the process of Confederation, begun in the middle of the nineteenth century and grown incrementally over the next four decades as most of the component pieces of the country were added. At Confederation in 1867, four "provinces" agreed to join to become Canada: Upper and Lower Canada (Quebec and Ontario), New Brunswick and Nova Scotia. By 1905, nine of the present ten provinces had joined, with only Newfoundland to follow in 1949.

From its first settlement to the end of the nineteenth century, Canada's wealth was concentrated in its hinterland. The First Nations hunted and gathered the bounty of the land. With the arrival of Europeans, furs and trees were harvested and transported for sale in European markets. The early explorers forged routes across the continent, eventually mapped by rigorous men like David Thompson and Simon Fraser, to siphon the goods to Atlantic ports for shipment to England and France. As such, the capacity to encompass territory was a critical economic activity, so the mapping and claiming of vast amounts of land became important. The more the better. And the relative harshness of the northern climate was not a particularly negative factor. In fact, it made animal fur thicker and more shiny.

Settlements in the early days, both native and European, were small and mobile. They tended to move where the commercial activity was. They moved to the mouths of eastern rivers to receive the logs that had been cut and floated downriver. And they moved to the points where rivers came together to serve trappers and traders. Only in the middle of the nineteenth century did any cities begin to develop, and they were relatively small. In 1850, Canada's biggest cities were Halifax, Montreal, Quebec City, and Toronto, ranging in population from

30,000 to 50,000. Of a total Canadian population of about 1.3 million, fewer than 20 percent lived in cities.

Some people, like David Thompson, lived in cities after a life in the wilderness, but their occupations drew them back to the countryside. Thompson did extensive surveying around the Great Lakes in his later years, but lived in Montreal before finding his final home in rural eastern Ontario.

Most people living in cities engaged in activities of commerce: supplying goods and services and providing investment capital for commercial activities.

From the first development of cities in Canada, urbanization has been the dominant trend. By the end of the twentieth century, the ratio of 80 percent rural to 20 percent urban had been inverted. In fact, half of Canadians now live in the great urban regions of Toronto, Montreal, and Vancouver; and, adding in the next seven cities by size, Canadian cities give home to three-quarters of the population.

Governments Lag Behind

Canada has become a predominantly urban nation. But you might not know it from listening to the political discourse in this country. An inspection of what they talk about in the federal parliament would lead you to believe this is still a largely rural country, dominated by logging (softwood lumber), cattle farming (mad cow disease), and grain farming (the Crow's Nest Pass Agreement and subsequent accords on grain shipping rates). There is little talk of the regulatory investment environment, HIV-AIDS, or urban transit. And an inspection of the provincial *Hansards* would not be much different.

And, in fact, the distribution of seats in the parliaments across the country shows a strong bias towards rural representation, with the average rural ridings having 30 percent fewer voters than the average urban constituency. The distribution of seats has not kept pace with the rate of people moving into cities.

It is the overwhelming choice of immigrants to Canada to live in a city—about half of them choose to live in the Toronto region, and most of the rest choose Vancouver, Montreal, or Ottawa. No wonder: in the cities they can find relatives, people who speak their language, housing, markets that sell the foods they prefer, and programs to facilitate their settlement in language, work training, and cultural adaptation; and, most importantly, they can find work. It is not that a smaller place couldn't offer some of these things, but very few places can offer the breadth and depth that large cities do. For example, former Winnipeg mayor Glen Murray wanted to increase that city's capacity to welcome immigrants, because he knew what a tremendous benefit they are to a community, but he left office before he could outfit the city appropriately.

The modern Canadian city is unconnected to the old Canadian myths of the wilderness. The Canada of furs, logs, wheat fields, canoes, and the cry of the loon at the lake has given way to the energized city of café and boulevard society, the opera, or a hip-hop concert. What passes for a day in the outdoors for many Canadians, and many new Canadians in particular, is spent at Burnaby Lake in Vancouver, on the Toronto Islands, or on Mount Royal in Montreal. The old Canadian tradition of quitting the city for the country, either to the cottage on a weekend or to a small town when the working life has finished, is receding. Instead, retired couples are finding lofts downtown, where they can walk to all the shops and markets they need, and find a wide range of places to eat, watch a show, or stroll in a park. In Toronto, they can ride the subway to a ravine park, walk for a couple of hours surrounded by trees, flowers, and grass, emerge on a city street for a coffee, and take the transit system back home. In Vancouver, they can walk for hours along the seashore, from the old Canadian Pacific train station on the inner harbour, around Stanley Park and False Creek, out to Kitsilano on English Bay, stopping at Granville Island on the way for lunch or coffee. The country in the city is the new trend, and Canadians love it.

If you look at who lives in Canada's large cities, it is increasingly people born outside of Canada, who have little sense of our wilderness history and mythology, except what they may have seen in a Canadian government travel poster or brochure. The official government depiction of Canada is still replete with the Rocky Mountains, lighthouses, and pristine lakes. But the newcomers come to Canada's cities, and particularly to Toronto, Vancouver, and Montreal. Their idea of Canada is urban and highly social. Part of this is practical. They know that the city is where opportunity abounds, and where they can find transitional help until they have found their feet. That isn't to say that they will not come to enjoy the non-urban parts of Canada, as do most Canadians from time to time, but they will come to it fresh, not with the baggage of myth.

This abandonment of the old myths is not merely symbolic. In fact, the economic nature of the country has changed dramatically. Canada's economy was founded on resource extraction—first the harvesting of furs and fish, then the removal of wood and minerals. The development of large grain farms on the prairie, the discovery of oil in Alberta and Saskatchewan, and the growth of a large cattle industry completed the picture that for many exists to this day, the picture of Canada as a place where wealth springs from nature. But a close look at Canadian economic figures shows that less than 5 percent of gross domestic product comes from these industries.

Since the end of the Second World War, the backbone of Canada's economy has been automobile manufacturing and house construction, both very much urban concerns. The growth of a large and dynamic automotive industry, first under the protection of British Preferential Tariffs, then the Canada–US Auto Pact, and finally through the attraction of the big Japanese manufacturers, has been critical to the economy. Much of that production has been in central Canada, where most Canadians live. And the growth of a powerful and skillful construction industry, in demand around the world, has been a critical economic factor. Canadian property developers and builders, and their attendant professions of planners, architects, and other service professionals, have built strong firms in Canada, but can also be found around the world wherever new homes and buildings are rising.

This shows that Canada's economy is now based on information and design, the benchmarks of modernity. Whether it is the clear stars like Bruce Mau conceiving the articulation plan for the Museum of Modern Art in New York, architect Jack Diamond designing the city hall in Jerusalem, planner Ken Greenberg overseeing the reclamation of urban space over the Big Dig in Boston, or Roch Voisine producing a blockbuster music CD in Nashville, Canadians are working around the world. Where can you see them? Get on a Friday afternoon Canada-bound flight at Heathrow, La Guardia, LAX, Milan, or Tokyo, and you'll see them—often in business class, thanks to their frequent-flyer upgrades—heading home for the weekend.

Or you'll see them at midweek, travelling to the world's financial capitals, because they work in the Canadian financial industries, developing internationally competitive products for investors and businesses. Leading Canadian investment managers like Burgundy Asset Management, Duncan Ross and Associates, and Gluskin Scheff perform with the world's best. Canadians are good at business, despite a harping and lamenting press. York University business professor James Gillies has noted for years that Canada has more millionaires per capita than any country in the world.

Part of the discussion about the old and new economy in Canada has to do with how wealth is created. The old-economy view is that the wealth is in the ground: in the oil, the wood, the ore, and the wheat. The new-economy view is that the wealth is only created by getting those things out of the ground, and to do that requires the assembly of pools of capital that can support the extraction enterprise. That assembly of capital is the stuff of business, and it is typically done in the financial capitals, the big cities. The old-economy view, supported by labour, is that the process is exploitive of the hinterland and of working people, that the enterprise takes too much out and leaves too little behind. The new economy says that what should be rewarded are the risking of capital and the designing of a system that turns wheat into bread at the market, oil into fuel at the gas pump, and wood into a beautiful new home.

In a sense, the world has left this debate between the new and old economies behind. The old economy now occupies a small percentage of our economic space and our people. A trip across downtown Toronto will find people occupied in teaching and learning at schools, universities, and hospitals, in the design of everything from chic clothing to financial products, and in the delivery of social programs to kids, the aged, and the infirm. And, interestingly, if you were to take a trip across rural Canada, you would find a significant portion of the population engaged in the same types of pursuits. You would find Ian Kennedy, an early retired school teacher living on the east coast of Vancouver Island, earning a living writing for rugby and motorcycle magazines; Denny Morrow of Yarmouth, Nova Scotia, who has made a career organizing co-operative associations for fishermen, canners, and woodlot owners; and Wendy Maxwell of Gambier Island, British Columbia, who has designed an effective and innovative way for children to learn French.

But while Canadians have moved easily and seamlessly into the new economy, their governments have lagged far behind in three ways: voter distribution has failed to keep pace with urbanization; our parliaments continue to talk about such old issues as Quebec separatism and western alienation; and there is a fiscal imbalance that neglects the important places cities have become.

O Canada

This book looks at how Canada has become one of the most urbanized countries in the world since Confederation, and looks at some of the gaps that have opened up as our governing structures, practices, and habits have failed to keep pace. It will look at some of the great capabilities we have in Canada, and discuss how leveraging them properly could make us even more successful as a country. Finally, it will articulate a vision for Canada in the twenty-first century that will optimize our strengths, and seek to resolve our weaknesses, to produce a great country.

Section One looks at the two great twentieth-century trends of urbanization and immigration, and how they have converged to create a country dominated by its large, economically vibrant and diverse urban regions. These two forces are each outlined in their own chapter, and the dynamic result is examined, especially from the perspective of a political system that seems to have been caught by surprise and rendered paralyzed. The concept of "control of destiny" is critical to the ability of cities to succeed, and this section establishes it as the critical imperative for Canada's international competitiveness.

Section Two breaks down the problem of our invisible or ignored cities into the component topics that must be addressed. A chapter looks at each of governance, powers, finance, and leadership. What governance structures can work best for which cities? What are the necessary powers for cities to have for control of destiny? Do our cities have adequate financial tools at hand to be able to fulfill the expectations of their citizens? The crucial role of leadership is examined, not only by asking what kinds of leaders we need, but by asking whether successful leaders can emerge under the current structures and restraints.

Section Three looks to the future and imagines what could be done. The first chapter in the section imagines a minor reshuffling of current conditions, which a hard-nosed realist might agree to. But that would not take Canada very far, so the second chapter looks at something bolder, an empowering of Vancouver, Toronto, and Montreal as effective "city states" within their regions, a development that would be possible without major constitutional change. The final chapter looks more boldly still into the future, and calls for a substantial rebuilding of the country, taking the view that we cannot any longer afford to be captives of our constitutional documents if we hope to be masters of our future. I propose a bold change with the creation of three city-provinces in Vancouver, Montreal, and Toronto, along with a major redrawing of provincial entities through Maritime Union and Prairie Union.

Urban Nation is an homage to Canada, the country I love. Chapter headings borrow lines from our national anthem, and from the poem by Robert Stanley Weir from which the anthem is drawn. My intent is the one phrase which I do not in fact use: true patriot love.

The Urban Trend across the Generations: Changing the Conversation

I grew up in the 1950s in Vancouver, then a city of half a million people on the western edge of the continent. My memories were urban: riding my bicycle on a sidewalk over the crunch of maple keys, playing football on a boulevard in a busy street, taking the bus down to the beach or to Ted Fraser's Book Bin, crossing the neighbourhood through laneways and backyards. As I dream, I think of long summer city days, of cars and buses, houses and gardens, and stores full of things to eat and read.

My father grew up in a town, in Brantford, Ontario, almost forty years before me. Many of his memories were urban, too, but they were balanced by a strong rural sense of his country. He spent his summers working at summer camps, and whenever he went away from Brantford, to school in Kingston, to Muskoka in the summers, he travelled slowly in the slow cars and over the narrow roads of the time, through slightly populated countryside. He remembered his time spent in canoes, camping by lakes, hearing the call of the loon, and fixing tires miles from any garage. But he moved to Toronto, then to Vancouver, and spent his life in a decidedly urban way: driving to work in downtown office buildings, talking on telephones, flying from airport to airport, and dancing to big bands in hotel ballrooms.

My sons have grown up in Toronto. Their lives have been very urban. The earliest safety lesson was to watch for cars. They learned to cross the one road at the end of our street, the only obstacle on their two-minute walk to the neighbourhood school. They began to take the bus and subway to school at age twelve; they meet their friends in bars, clubs, and coffee shops; they will become knowledge workers, adept at using computers and electronic tools to deal with issues and problems; and they have a very high tolerance for difference.

These three generations of men in my family span about a hundred years as I write this. This is roughly the period of time when Canada became highly urbanized, when we virtually lost our dependence on and connection to the land, and when we became one of the most successful countries in the world. Being born near the middle of the twentieth century in Canada, I was a lucky beneficiary of this process of urbanization, which carried with it a burgeoning of wealth, health, security, and safety, education, democracy, equity, opportunity, and joy unsurpassed anywhere. Not a perfect country—not yet—but certainly near a pinnacle of comparative achievement in the history of this planet.

Over those three generations of men in my family, the conversation on cities has changed. My oldest son's first job after university was with the British Columbia government's municipal affairs branch, working on the fiscal arrangements between municipalities and the province. His brother wrote a paper on cities in his graduating year at McMaster University in Hamilton, Ontario. In his Public Administration classes at the University of Victoria, they talk about cities the way they talk about nations and provinces. The national conversation has begun to change, perhaps well after the country has changed. People have been far ahead of their governments in becoming urban. They've voted with their feet, their interests, and in many cases their hearts. Governments are just beginning to take note.

1

WE SEE THEE RISE
From Forest to Farm to City

Even at the start of the twenty-first century, tourism ads prepared by the federal and provincial governments in Canada feature images of lighthouses, wheat fields, and icebergs. Rare are the images of city festivals, concerts, gourmet restaurants, or city parks. The purveyed image is still that of the hinterland, and the city is a mere flyover.

Was Canada ever truly characterized by wilderness and rural imagery? Was the lived experience of a majority of people in this land non-urban? Much of the history of Canada has been written as if it were. Our early accounts of Europeans in Canada recount the trips of explorers from the Atlantic coast deep into the hinterlands in search of furs, a route to the Pacific, and riches. The settlements of the time are little mentioned or commented on; indeed, they are treated mostly as provisioning sites for the unrelenting forays into the wild.

But the population numbers that we have indicate that the cities and towns of the sixteenth, seventeenth, and eighteenth centuries may have held the majority of the population. While explorers like Samuel de Champlain penetrated deep into the continent, discovering wealth and mapping geography, he also created Quebec City, which has thrived for four hundred years.

From the days of Cartier in the early sixteenth century to those of Champlain in the first half of the seventeenth, there was not very much settlement. For Europeans, North America was a source of wealth, not a future home. Few of the fur traders even did their own trapping. Rather, they traded with Native trappers and the odd European who had taken to the bush to mount trapping operations.

The cities that developed in the age of exploration were agents of empire, administrative and commercial outposts that acted as vital links between France or Britain and the New World. They were places where officials could organize the commercial activities of the day, whether it be cod fishing or transshipment of beaver pelts. The first was St. John's, Newfoundland, into whose harbour John Cabot sailed in 1497 and which became a standard haven for European fishermen thereafter. But no real settlement developed there for most of the sixteenth century; it was merely a point of respite from the volatile Atlantic Ocean. As was Louisbourg on Cape Breton Island, which thrived for almost forty years before its administrative and military purpose was taken away and it collapsed.

Quebec City, founded by Samuel de Champlain in 1608, did endure, but its early history was not dissimilar to that of Louisbourg. Nor was that of Montreal, founded by Paul de Chomedey de Maisonneuve in 1642. In their early years, both acted as commercial and administrative centres, primarily for the fur trade. There was little sustainable commercial activity being carried on in these towns, and they grew very slowly. They developed services that towns and cities need, most famously Jeanne Mance's creation of a hospital in Montreal. And they developed some small businesses that specialized in things it didn't make sense to do in homes, such as blacksmithing, distilling, and printing.

But the main purpose of these places was to receive ships from France, which would be laden with supplies to sustain the colonial communities, and from the other direction to receive canoe-loads of furs from the hinterland to be loaded into the ships returning to France. The supplies from France were comprehensive, including foodstuffs, wine, furniture, medical supplies and instruments, books, clothing, and tools. And there was also a massive array of goods to be carried in the canoes back into the hinterland to trade with the natives and others who were actually collecting the furs.

A further look into the interior of the continent would reveal scaled-down versions of these settlements. Places like York Factory, Albany Factory, and Grand Portage were principal trading points, often housing twenty-five to fifty people—the trading agents and their families—and beyond them, along a network of lakes and rivers, were smaller places where further exchanges would take place. These were more mobile stations, which might relocate in response to the moves of the trappers and their quarry. In 1700, there were probably a thousand men engaged in moving canoes back and forth along the supply chain. The population of Quebec City was 2,000.

Perhaps the best way to look at these settlements is as points in a very long supply chain that had, at its centre, Paris. A map of that supply chain would be a series of strings extending out into the world, each bringing back some particular item in demand in the courts of the aristocracy. From Asia, it might be silk; from Africa, spices; from northern Europe, textiles; and from "the New World," furs. The fur trade string extended from Paris to La Rochelle to Quebec City to Grande Portage to a string of forts that moved along waterways and across lakes, at each point separating into smaller strands that reached more variously and tenuously into the wilderness of the vast continent. Those strands rarely connected to one another in a weblike way, but were linearly connected to form the most direct supply channel. It was the string, not the territory through which it extended, that was important. It was classic imperialism: the hinterland existed to supply the centre.

The Industrial Revolution

This period lasted until about 1800. Two things changed it. The first was what Jane Jacobs described as "import replacement." That happens when someone, rather than buying and waiting for someone to send a table from London or Paris, looks for someone to make it locally. This spurs local commerce and creates local markets, and people begin to build furniture factories, textile mills, and tailor shops.

The second instrument for change was the development of the steam engine, which James Watt perfected and put into manufacture in the last years of the eighteenth century. Robert Fulton built and operated the first commercially successful steamship service on the Hudson River between Albany and New York City in 1807, a signal moment in the application of steam power. This led to the Industrial Revolution, which expanded manufacturing by making tasks easier and facilitated transportation by releasing ships from the fickle winds and enabled the overland shipment of goods and people via railroads. Why wait a year or more for a new dining room table and chairs to arrive from Europe when you could have it in a few months from a factory in Montreal, delivered to your home by rail and wagon? And, if you were that furniture maker, why not think about selling your goods into Quebec City, Kingston, or New York City, now that you could get them there reliably?

Railway building in North America lagged behind that in Britain, but from 1836, when the Champlain and Saint Lawrence Railroad opened between Montreal and Lake Champlain (from whence travellers could take a boat across the lake and down the Hudson River to New York City), for the next forty years a great number of short railways opened.

This railroad building reached its dramatic crescendo in the construction of the great Canadian project, the Canadian Pacific Railway. It was the completion of the CPR that made the country; indeed, it was a requirement of the government of British Columbia when it agreed to join Confederation in 1871. The work began in earnest in 1880 and was completed in late 1885, with the first transcontinental train running between Montreal and Port Moody, BC, in June 1886.

All this railroad construction required steel, wood, fuel, locomotives and cars, and workers. And once they were open for business, they carried travellers who required hotels, food, ancillary transportation, and a whole array of other goods and services, all of which clustered around railway stations in cities. The railways built cities and economies.

Import replacement and the Industrial Revolution had a profound effect on where people decided to live. As manufacturing facilities rose up, workers wanted to live near them. And suppliers and distributors wanted to situate near them. Proximity became an asset, and so towns began to grow with an agglomeration of factories, housing, and the shops and commercial establishments that supplied them and their workers.

This growth was quite spontaneous, a response to the possibilities offered by new technology and to the inefficiencies of colonial supply. Unlike the previous growth of cities and towns, this was directed not by administrative decree from outside, but by a natural response to opportunity and need. Jane Jacobs, among others, has noted this seeming "accidental" quality in the growth of cities. It is in responding to the desires and needs of people that the most interesting and sustainable cities, and the most vibrant parts of those cities, have developed. Jacobs has observed that when central planners set out to decree what shall be, they often get it wrong. But when cities grow more "organically" in response to demands, and are allowed to change and alter their nature as those demands change, what results is more enduring.

Farm Begat City, or Vice Versa?

By 1900, Canada's population was about five million. Montreal was the biggest city, with just over a quarter million people. It was stated commonly that over 80 percent of Canadians "live on farms" or are "rural," a figure that, a century later, was to reverse itself, with 80 percent living in cities. But it is worth looking at that 1900 statistic, and considering what it actually means. In fact, the line between farm and town was not sharply etched.

The bulk of the farms of the time were small family farms, and many of them clustered together in farming communities, the centre of which was a farm town that acted as a local commercial and social centre. It would be a number of years before the developments of agricultural technology permitted the creation of large farms that could be worked by a small workforce with powerful machinery at hand. Farms were often close to, and vitally linked to, the needs of cities and towns, where the demand for their goods resided. When technology spurred farm consolidations, there was an exodus of farmers and their children to the cities, often to fill jobs in factories.

The First Wave of Urbanization: Country to City

The building of the railroads kicked the Industrial Revolution into gear in Canada. The political stability brought about by Confederation in 1867, the ambition of Sir John A. Macdonald to create a thriving country, and the availability of new technology all came together in the building of the transcontinental railroad. The railroad itself demanded an enormous volume of manufactured products. And the army of men constructing it created a demand for goods that would sustain them.

And in 1879, Macdonald brought in the National Policy, which featured protective tariffs to spur domestic manufacture. Before the House of Commons, Macdonald moved "the adoption of a National Policy, which, by a judicious readjustment of the Tariff, will benefit and foster the agricultural, the mining, the manufacturing and other interest of the Dominion." New tariff barriers encouraged food processing, lumber production, and a whole range of products for the home, in order to create employment, "restore prosperity to our struggling industries," and stimulate interprovincial trade.

The results showed immediately in what were to become the country's key industrial cities. From 1881 to 1891, the population of Toronto jumped by 88 percent. Montreal grew by 40 percent, Hamilton 36 percent. In the west, Winnipeg increased over 220 percent and Victoria 185 percent.

Thus began Canada's first great wave of urbanization. It was in the last decades of the nineteenth century, and the first half of the twentieth, that people began to populate cities in a deliberate and obvious way. These were, for the most part, the small regional cities. Some farm towns became bigger towns, and then regional cities, like London, Ontario. Many towns grew up along the CPR line, like Moose Jaw, Saskatchewan, which started as a depot for railroad building crews and by 1915 had almost 15,000 people.

Looking at a series of maps of Canada from 1900 to 1950, one would see in each decade the presence of more cities of significant population, and would see those cities growing. Some grew slowly, particularly those in the Maritime provinces whose economies had already been established when the wave of European immigration passed over the region. In Quebec and Ontario, the major cities of Quebec, Montreal, and Toronto were clearly established, but a whole other set of cities grew up: Saint-Laurent and Lachine, which became part of an expanding Montreal; Weston, Long Branch, and Mimico, which became part of Toronto as it grew; and cities that still stand independently like Hamilton, Guelph, and Windsor. In the west, cities grew anew as the region first became populated by farmers and railway workers, then began to develop commercial and government centres, often along the rail lines. First, they appeared along the CPR in the south (Winnipeg, Regina, Moose Jaw, Calgary, Port Moody, Vancouver), and later along the CNR in the north (Saskatoon, Edmonton, Prince George).

The residents of these cities were immigrants and in-migrants, those who had moved from within Canada to one of the cities. They moved for a number of reasons. Work was the main one. Jobs were to be found in the cities, in the new factories and stores, and related commercial opportunities abounded. Teachers, nurses, doctors, lawyers, clerks, accountants, and bookkeepers were all needed. People also moved to town for education, so that they could begin to fill some of these jobs the new economy required. And they often moved because life in the city was not as hard as life on the farm or in the hinterland. Rural life was hard, with unrelenting demands and little forgiveness. Failure to take in a crop, or chop a winter wood supply, or seed at the right time, or tend cattle, could have disastrous results. Farmers were locked into the rigid demands of the seasons, the weather, and the independent nature of living plants and animals. In the city, there was a little respite, a chance to take a breather.

Cities of the time grew on fairly compact footprints. Proximity was useful, and transportation was first of all by foot, then horse, and then often a public conveyance. It is clear today in looking at our older cities that the cores are quite compact and dense, with narrow streets and buildings coming right up to the sidewalks. One can look at cities like Quebec City, Montreal, Toronto, and Vancouver and read them almost as one would read a cross-section of a tree. The older rings at the centre are close together, while the more recent rings on the outside are more widely spaced. That compactness aided communication, transportation, and the flow of commerce.

Everything got built close to everything else. Factories were near homes, homes were near stores, stores were near the business centre. One of the signs of urbanization was the building of transit systems—initially, horse-drawn street railways that were subsequently electrified. The earliest horse-drawn rail systems were in Toronto and Montreal (1861), Quebec City (1865), Halifax (1866), and Saint John (1869). Electrification came in the 1890s, reducing the need for large horse stabling operations throughout town and increasing the power of the systems. Much of the work was done by private investors, who saw a chance to make profits. By World War I there were about fifty systems in Canada, in places like Brandon, Manitoba, and Brantford, Ontario, in St. Albert, Alberta, and St. Stephen, New Brunswick. All of the street rail systems, with the exception of Toronto's, were terminated between 1945 and 1955, giving way to gas-powered buses, except in the odd place like Vancouver where electric trolley buses dominate in the older parts of the city.

The list of the cities that built street railways is an interesting one. All of them were "urbanized" enough to install systems in the decades around the turn of the twentieth century. With the odd exception such as Ridgeway–Crystal Beach and Lake Louise, this is a list of the important cities that built up in the first half of the twentieth century in Canada. All of the twenty biggest cities in Canada in 2001 are on this list, except Saskatoon.

Belleville, Ontario	Moncton, New Brunswick	Sarnia, Ontario
Brandon, Manitoba	Montreal, Quebec	Saskatoon, Saskatchewan
Brantford, Ontario	Moose Jaw, Saskatchewan	Sault Ste. Marie, Ontario
Calgary, Alberta	Nelson, British Columbia	Sherbrooke, Quebec
Chatham, Ontario	Niagara Falls, Ontario	Sudbury, Ontario
Cornwall, Ontario	Oshawa, Ontario	Sydney, Nova Scotia
Edmonton, Alberta	Ottawa, Ontario	Thunder Bay, Ontario
Guelph, Ontario	Peterborough, Ontario	Toronto, Ontario
Halifax, Nova Scotia	Quebec City, Quebec	Trois-Rivières, Quebec
Hamilton, Ontario	Regina, Saskatchewan	Vancouver, British Columbia
Hull (Gatineau), Quebec	Ridgeway—Crystal Beach, Ontario	Victoria, British Columbia
Kingston, Ontario	St. Albert, Alberta	Welland, Ontario
Kitchener-Waterloo, Ontario	St. Catharines, Ontario	Windsor, Ontario
Lake Louise, Alberta	Saint John, New Brunswick	Winnipeg, Manitoba
Lethbridge, Alberta	St. John's, Newfoundland	Whitehorse, Yukon
Lévis, Quebec	St. Stephen, New Brunswick	Yarmouth, Nova Scotia
London, Ontario	St. Thomas, Ontario	

(Derived from Internet list posted by David A. Wyatt of the University of Manitoba, assisted by Ray F. Corley of Scarborough, Ontario.)

This process of urbanization was abetted considerably by the First World War. The industrial effort needed to support the war increased both the amount of manufacturing and the number of factory workers, people who became trained and experienced in factory work. It also took a number of young men from rural Canada to fight in Europe, leaving those behind on the farms to find a way to make their operations work with fewer men. And when a lot of those soldiers returned to Canada after the war, they didn't go back to the farms and villages, but found work in the cities.

This rapid industrialization created a large working class in the cities, and a large demand for housing, transportation, and a broad range of goods, all of which increased production. Investors flocked to new entrepreneurial opportunities, and capitalism became widely appealing, attracting not only the traditional big money men, but small investors interested in buying shares in new enterprises. Most of them would have a nasty surprise in 1929 with the collapse of the equity markets and the advent of a decade of depression, but in the early 1920s there was a tremendous expansion of prosperity.

In the large cities, buildings were built taller and bigger. Skyscrapers appeared across the country. The Bank of Commerce tower in Toronto, built in 1930 with thirty-four floors, was the tallest building in the British Commonwealth until 1962. Factories were developed on a scale not seen before. They can still be seen in city centres, now often converted to residential uses, in Vancouver's Yaletown, Montreal's *vieille ville* by the river, Toronto's Queen Street West corridor, and Victoria's inner harbour. Neighbourhoods sprang up around these city cores, and as the city grew it would replace houses with commercial and industrial buildings.

At the same time, suburbs developed in the desirable countryside around the city centre. Some of these, like Shaughnessy in Vancouver, were generated by the Canadian Pacific Railway on land it had been granted as part of the contract for building the railway—in effect, its future consideration. Others were built by a variety of private developers and speculators, in response to a desire of some, usually wealthier people, to be outside the commotion of the city. These are the close-in residential neighbourhoods that now tend to be highly valued, with large, well-built houses, gracious, tree-lined streets, and relatively easy connections to downtown. Vancouver's Shaughnessy, Toronto's Deer Park and Forest Hill, Montreal's Westmount, Ottawa's Rockcliffe, and Edmonton's Strathcona fill this bill. Rail lines were often built out to these suburbs, either by the developer of the subdivision or an entrepreneur who hoped to profit. They were seldom built by governments.

Cities continued to build even during the depression of the 1930s and World War II. The essential building of the downtown cores carried on, the spaces between the rural subdivisions and the central city filled in, and a newer, less dense kind of suburb began. The growth rates of cities varied year to year, and from city to city, but in the 1940s, particularly after the war, they increased from 3 to 9 percent annually; in the 1950s from 4 to 6 percent; and in the 1960s from 2 to 4 percent. Taken cumulatively, this was significant growth; by the end of each decade those cities were looking at increases of anywhere from 25 to 50 percent, all needing places to live, work, shop, and learn.

Sprawl: Spilling over at the Edges

Particularly after the end of the war, there was an apparent and dramatic change in the look of urban development, and it was due to the automobile and truck. Automobiles had been growing in popularity and becoming more available for decades, but after the war and into the 1950s they became ubiquitous. They were attractive, increasingly affordable, and liberating. They became status symbols as well. They became a bulwark of the economy. Vehicle manufacturing and house construction were the twin pillars of the Canadian economy in the second half of the twentieth century.

And they transformed the urban landscape, enabling the building of suburbs farther away from the centre of the city, which resulted in the building of a web of roads that were endlessly widened or supplemented. This was the serious advent of what became known as "sprawl," the continuous growth of cities into neighbouring areas, taking over farm and forest for the building of subdivisions—what folksinger Pete Seeger called row upon row of "little boxes on the hillside" (a song written by Malvina Reynolds). At the time, there was relatively little criticism of sprawl. It was seen as a natural way to grow, and it was heartily supported by the marketing efforts of the property developers and the car manufacturers who argued they were giving people what they wanted. The fact that public budgets were providing huge amounts to build the road and utility connections to these new subdivisions, and that automobiles were significant polluters, were neither apparent nor part of the public discourse. And so the suburbs grew like topsy, oriented to and dependent on the car. Sprawl continues to the present day, subsidized on a massive scale by the public sector, which provides roads and other infrastructure. The patterns of land use, even the nature and style of the houses being built, have varied little.

These patterns can be seen across Canada, and indeed in most developed countries. Where the city is over a century old, there is a downtown core often with a ring of older factories, often along the sea, lake, or river front, then a succession of suburbs, some of which are now inner-city residential neighbourhoods. Newer cities, like some in the southwestern US, including Phoenix, seem to be all suburbs and completely car-centred. There may be a smattering of older buildings, but the streets are wide, while the central city contains little residential accommodation and dies at the end of the work day. Some, Phoenix being one, are trying to invent a central city by building cultural and sport facilities downtown, and Phoenix is even installing an urban rail line.

During this first phase of urbanization, spurred by the transformation of the Canadian economy from one based primarily on resource extraction, fishing, and farming to one that had a significant manufacturing capability, Canada went from being dominated by a few significantly large cities like Quebec City, Montreal, Halifax, and

Toronto, to having a larger number of thriving regional cities, all of which had hopes of becoming metropolises.

The Second Wave: Small City to Big City

What happened next, though, was very different. Rather than the continued growth of these regional cities, Canada had a second phase of urbanization that saw the growth of a relative few places in part at the expense of those hopeful regional cities. This was driven by two things: increased and sustained immigration and a further transformation of the economy.

The period from 1950 to 1985 saw a steady and high level of immigration, much of it from postwar Europe but increasingly from other places. The years since 1985 have seen an even higher annual intake, and they came from everywhere. What was entirely clear was that they tended to come from cities, and they wanted to go to cities. What is even clearer is that they came from big cities and wanted to go to big cities. They were urban and metropolitan. Immigration is discussed more fully in the next chapter.

The other change was in the economy, which developed a strong component of information and design. Entertainment became important, as people wanted to consume films, television shows, music, magazines and books, and sporting events. Making better goods and services, and then promoting these improvements to consumers, became crucial competitive factors. Designing a better car, dress, television sitcom, typewriter, or even a program to house the homeless, required a lot of effort. And communicating how much better these things were became a key job that employed many. Virtually all of these jobs were in cities, and they were increasingly found in the bigger cities, the commercial hubs.

Mounting all of these efforts depended on financial capital, and bigger cities are where they money is. Of course it was always true, even in the days of the fur trade. There had to be money with which to acquire and equip the ships that left from French coastal towns, to fill them with stores and trading goods, to pay the crews, to build the New World settlements that anchored the fur trade, to acquire the canoes and crews that ventured into the hinterlands, and to ship the pelts back to European markets. There had to be capital later on to build the roads and docks, the railways, the factories, houses, and shops, to fund the start-up of the radio and television stations or the making of a motion picture, or to hire the programmers to develop a new software product.

Originally, capital came from the courts of Europe, then from syndicates of investors and a variety of financial schemes. Eventually, banks were organized and equity markets developed. But all of them tended to be centred in cities—in Paris, London, and Amsterdam, then in New York, Boston, Montreal, and Toronto. In the nineteenth century and the first three-quarters of the twentieth century, Montreal was the financial capital of Canada. St. James Street in Montreal was the centre of Canadian commerce, and the big companies of the day were headquartered there. In response to the terrorist activities of the 1960s and the election of the separatist Parti Québécois in 1976, the commercial centre of Canada shifted to Toronto, which also took over Montreal's long-standing status as Canada's most populous city.

As the information economy developed, it became apparent that the greatest competitive advantage was a high level of human capital. Human capital is a term that encompasses the education, training, and adaptive ability of a person to be an effective participant in society, usually in relation to the labour market. The competitive capacity of countries has long been analyzed in terms of financial capital; in the last forty years other categories have been added: human capital, social capital (the social cohesion and resilience of a society), and most recently natural capital (environmental attributes and sustainability). In order to be competitive with other nations and economies, it became important for countries to invest in the education and training of their people. In the developed world this resulted in a spate of university and college development. There was a concerted and for the most part successful effort to increase the percentage of people getting education past high school from something under 10 percent to at least a quarter or a third of the population.

Most of this building took place in cities, and the biggest enrollment increases took place in the biggest cities, although this did cause some unease among governments. For reasons stated in another chapter, governments have not been comfortable with their biggest cities. There remains a rural and small-town bias in our legislative chambers. Ontario is a good example, particularly during the boom in the construction of universities and colleges in the 1960s and '70s. Ontario premier Bill Davis was a strong visionary on education, as had been his predecessor, John Robarts. Davis was elected in the riding of Brampton, a small city northwest of Toronto that had long since become contiguous as the two places sprawled together. Davis could never bring himself to identify as being related to Toronto; he was always Bill Davis from Brampton. Before becoming premier, he served as education minister for almost a decade. Following, and building on, the lead of Leslie Frost and John Robarts, he vigorously expanded the postsecondary system, making sure that every part of the province was served. Thunder Bay got Lakehead University in 1965, St. Catharines got Brock in 1964, Sudbury got Laurentian in 1957, and Peterborough got Trent in 1965. Toronto got York University in 1959, and Waterloo University was established in Kitchener-Waterloo in 1957; both of these have grown into large, internationally known institutions. In addition, over twenty community colleges were started, scattered around the province, including smaller centres like North Bay, Barrie, Welland, Sarnia, and Sault Ste. Marie.

But the universities and colleges with the largest enrollments are in the big cities in Canada. According to statistics from the Association of Universities and Colleges of Canada, 35 percent of full-time and 40 percent of part-time university students go to schools in Toronto, Montreal, or Vancouver, the three biggest cities. Schools in the nine largest cities account for 56 percent of both full- and part-time students. The biggest universities are University of Toronto, with 63,000 full-time students; York, with 42,000; Université de Montréal with 38,000; UBC with 33,000; and University of Alberta, in Edmonton, with 32,000. All of these are located in one of five Canadian cities with populations over a million.

And with the exception of Queen's University in Kingston, Ontario, all of the Canadian universities that rank internationally are in our fifteen largest cities, and most of them are in our top ten. So students interested in studying at the best schools will tend towards one of our big cities.

And what happens in the university world happens in most other walks of life. Journalists often begin their careers at small-city newspapers or radio or television stations, but as their careers progress they move to bigger markets and end up in Toronto or Vancouver. People working in the financial industries move to where the bigger deals and bigger clients are—again, one of the large cities. Athletes and entertainers also move to the big markets in the big cities.

Size Begets Size: The Regional City

And this accumulation tends to build on itself, as the critical mass becomes sufficient at some point to begin to exert its own gravity, and people seeking greater success cannot avoid the move. The Toronto region accounted for about 25 percent of the Canadian population in 2005. By 2020 it will account for about 30 percent, and that figure will keep on rising. So will the percentage figures of Montreal and Vancouver, although they will rise at slower rates, and even they will likely lose some people who are seeking to get ahead in their careers to Toronto. Of course, Toronto will lose individuals to other places, too: those who are on the final legs of careers and who seek better weather, lower housing prices, a slower pace of life, or proximity to distant family members.

This seeming ascendancy of Toronto is not a testament to Toronto's superiority as a place, or to any distinctive natural attributes it has. It is a phenomenon of large, leading cities in a region, and in a country. Montreal was once dominant in Canada, as mentioned earlier, but lost that position through a series of political decisions taken by the provincial government. What has happened in Toronto could have happened in another city had it been differently positioned by geography and history. But Toronto was in the right place—the Great Lakes—at the right time, the rapid industrialization of North America centred on the Great Lakes. And it helped that it was in a sovereign jurisdiction, Ontario, that could adopt policies that allowed it to succeed against the competitor cities of the region, Detroit, Cleveland, Buffalo, and Rochester. As Chicago dominated the western Great Lakes, and New York the Atlantic Seaboard, so Toronto came to dominate the eastern Great Lakes.

And as in New York, Los Angeles, and Chicago in the US, London in the UK, Paris in France, Frankfurt in Germany, and Milan in Italy, growth tends to focus and concentrate in one regional city, and in Canada that has been Toronto. A measure of that difference is expressed in the world city rankings compiled by Loughborough

University's World and Global Cities project. It uses the presence of international business services firms like accountants and lawyers as a proxy for economic vitality, and presumes that economic vitality spins off social and cultural vitality. In their 1999 list, Toronto ranked tenth in the world, classified as a Beta World City, below the rank of the Alpha cities. In the 2004 ranking, it had moved up into the Alpha category, at seventh place, sitting just below the top cities that repeated from 1999: London, New York, Hong Kong, Paris, Tokyo, and Singapore. Montreal, which would have ranked about twenty-fifth in 1999, is not mentioned in 2004. Neither are Vancouver or Calgary, which appeared in the high 70s and 80s respectively in 1999. No other Canadian city is mentioned.

Canadian governments have not been happy with this trend, for a number of reasons. Quite rightly, they don't like the idea of the hollowing out of the country, leaving a few very large centres with vast areas containing stagnant or shrinking cities. And rural areas are over-represented in the federal parliament: the average constituency has about 100,000 voters, but a rural constituency has only 85,000, compared with 120,000 in an urban one. The provincial legislatures reflect the same bias. Some of this is due to a lag in responding to rapid urbanization, but the bias remains, and so parliamentarians try to stay the forces of urbanization by a variety of means.

They distribute government services to smaller centres, so the Ontario health insurance service offices are in Kingston. They construct elaborate schemes to take wealth generated in urban regions and distribute it in less wealthy areas, often propping up commercial activities in order to keep local employment. The Atlantic Institute for Market Studies has railed against these schemes for the Maritimes for years, saying they have a disempowering effect of creating dependency and sapping initiative. Governments use differential tax rates between jurisdictions—for instance, having higher education taxes in a large city—or they will take school tax revenue generated in one city and spend it in the rural areas.

It is not only governments that are unhappy with the strong gravitational pull of the big cities. Some environmentalists are as well, claiming that cities are despoilers of air and water. In fact, the average urban dweller has a smaller environmental footprint than a suburban or rural resident, due to their living in more confined spaces, walking or taking transit more often, and driving less. Some immigration critics, like Daniel Stoffman, lament the preference of immigrants for the big cities because, in their view, big cities are the cause of big problems in society, and the bigger they get the worse they get. It is true that big cities attract everyone, including the disadvantaged, who can find services and shelter at scale. But comparative crime rates show that cities are safer than rural areas, and city dwellers are healthier.

The People's Choice

The fact is that urbanization, like immigration, is a powerful trend driven by positive attraction, and that no amount of intervention will hold it back. People move to cities because they are more likely to find good jobs, strong social connections, cultural amenities, joy, and love. By their size alone, cities are apt to be able to offer all these things in a variety of ways. The complexity of urban economies produces a vast array of jobs, and the broad range of city inhabitants from across the country and around the world offers the opportunity for social interaction that is wide and deep. It is in the big cities that one can find a great variety of cultural activity, from opera to professional baseball, from live theatre to a big automotive show, from jazz clubs to literary festivals, from chamber music to rock concerts. You can find many of these things in smaller centres, but not on the scale and with the same variety as in the big cities, and people find that attractive.

Canada's two waves of urbanization—the first of which populated the towns and cities across the country as a response to the Industrial Revolution, and the second of which propelled the biggest of our cities forward—have left the country as one of the most urbanized nations in the world at the start of the twenty-first century. Our three metropolitan regions of Toronto, Montreal, and Vancouver are continuing to grow at a hearty pace. The next group of cities, including Edmonton, Calgary, Winnipeg, Hamilton, Ottawa, and Quebec City, continue to grow, but the gap between them and the metropolitan regions will continue to widen. And the cities below them will also experience a widening gap, some of them actually losing population as the century goes on.

These waves of urbanization have left a country dramatically different than the one that was formally established in 1867. And that difference was profoundly impacted by the other great trend: immigration. The question for Canada would be whether it could respond to its new character, or whether it would let the structures and practices of the past imprison it.

2

FROM FAR AND WIDE
The Changing Complexion of Canada

Immigrants began to arrive in Halifax, and other Atlantic ports, almost from the time of discovery and settlement in the sixteenth century. But the pace accelerated in the early nineteenth century, as settlers began to arrive from Great Britain. Highland Scots leaving through Greenock (Glasgow), Leith (Edinburgh), and Aberdeen; Irish leaving from Londonderry, Cork, Dublin, Belfast, and Waterford; English from London, Liverpool, and Plymouth; and even Welsh from Carmarthen arrived in Halifax. The voyages in the "ships" and brigs of the time were long, usually lasting between forty and fifty days, but occasionally as long as eighty days. Some ships were lost at sea, everyone on board perishing. And those who arrived were often in rough shape from the voyage, wracked by seasickness, weakened by relative confinement, and perhaps a bit stir-crazy from cramped ship conditions.

Many were "farmers and mechanics," as listed in ships' lists at the time, and settled for the most part in surrounding areas. Some were decommissioned soldiers given plots of land to settle. Many were virtually indigent, with no contacts in their new land, no money, and no resources. Colonial governors of the day were hard pressed to provide for these newcomers and were given to petitioning London for increased resources.

Some immigrants quickly moved deeper into the continent, continuing by ship, usually a coastal schooner, into the Gulf of St. Lawrence and on up the great river itself to Quebec City and Montreal. Many settled in Nova Scotia. The colonial government offered plots of land to many of the immigrants, particularly former soldiers, along the routes of proposed roads to places like Annapolis or Truro.

Over our history, from the first voyage of Jacques Cartier up the St. Lawrence in 1534 to the most recent landing at Pearson Airport in Toronto, immigration has been irregular and sporadic. For long periods of time, only small numbers of people arrived—indeed, for the early settlement period, the numbers were remarkably small—and then there would be a spurt.

From Cartier—who never really made an effort at settlement, although he did survive several harsh winters on the north shore of the St. Lawrence—to Samuel de Champlain's establishment of Quebec City in 1608, European arrivals were mostly itinerant traders bent on discovering and extracting the riches of the land. In 1635, there were eighty-five settlers in New France; in 1641, when Paul de Chomedey de Maisonneuve founded Montreal, three hundred; and by 1663, 2,500. One hundred and fifty years later, the population of New France was only 60,000, with only another 10,000 or so in the rest of the country. Even after the great battle on the Plains of Abraham in Quebec City in 1759, when the British defeated the French and triggered the retreat of France from North America, immigration did not accelerate much.

What is noticeable from looking at the yearly figures, though, is that there were spurts, and they were often driven by events in the country of origin. The breaking up of the Scottish clans in about 1745 resulted in the arrival of Scottish settlers in the Maritimes. The British–

American war (the American Revolution) resulted in a significant movement of British loyalists into Canada from about 1750 to 1780, in anticipation of the war, and in its aftermath and the creation of the new republic, the United States of America. The Highland Clearances in Scotland, when peasants were forced off the land so that it could be consolidated into large baronial estates, began in 1807 and spurred another wave of Scots arriving in Canada, this time pushing farther west into Quebec and Ontario. And the great famine in Ireland in 1846 drove many Irish out of the country, looking for a new life elsewhere, and Canada was a great recipient of their emigration.

The War of 1812 also acted as a great spur. As the British governors began to mount the defence of Upper and Lower Canada, the small Canadian population suddenly seemed to be a great vulnerability as they counted the potential recruits. An active recruitment of immigrants was conducted by the governors of the time, using land grants and other concessions as lures. It worked in attracting immigrants from Europe, and also from the United States.

The First Surge

Each of these events resulted in a brief spike in immigration. But it was not until the early twentieth century that the first dramatic increase took place. Taking power in 1896, the government of Sir Wilfrid Laurier looked west of central Ontario and saw a vast expanse of sparsely populated land. It was vulnerable to the "manifest destiny" aspirations of the United States. Despite the completion of the Canadian Pacific Railway, the land was still largely unoccupied.

Laurier had drafted the Ontario-born Manitoban Clifford Sifton into his cabinet, having collaborated with Sifton and Manitoba premier Thomas Greenway during the 1896 election. Sifton was a lawyer in Brandon, with extensive experience in real estate law and an abiding interest in politics. After a successful career in the Manitoba legislature, he moved to Ottawa and took on a number of tasks for Laurier, but none more famous and long-lasting than the great effort to populate the west.

Sifton did two main things as minister of the Interior, one internal and one external. Internally, he changed the incentives for immigration officers. Rather than paying them a salary, he paid them on commission, on the basis of how many immigrants they could attract. This made them much more ambitious and aggressive in recruiting immigrants.

Externally, he mounted a relentless and seemingly ubiquitous marketing campaign. Initially, he aimed it at the United States, where he knew there were former Canadians as well as a cohort of farmers experienced in cold-weather farming. Both groups would bring hard assets with them from their current farms. Less successfully, he targeted British farmers, but the main uptake from Britain was by people who wanted to move to cities.

But he also aimed at northern Europe, and there he struck pay dirt. Thousands of European farmers settled in the prairies in the first decade of the century. In those target countries, Canada seemed to be everywhere. Accounts of the time said you couldn't pass a lamp post in any rural village without seeing Canadian recruitment posters. It was one of the great marketing campaigns of the time.

To attract them, Sifton made land available either cheaply, or in some cases as land grants. The railway was expanded to provide dependable transportation of crops to markets, the railway companies were encouraged to free up some of their holdings for settlement, rates were stabilized by pacts like the Crow's Nest Pass Agreement, and the new farmers were attended to in any way that would likely lead to their successful immigration.

And the numbers showed the success of the program. From 1891 to 1902, before the effects of the program really kicked in, 437,830 immigrants arrived. From 1903 to 1914, 2,677,319 arrived, a sixfold increase. Even within these twelve-year periods, the numbers are spiky: more than a quarter-million in 1906 and 1910–13, with about 400,000 each in 1912 and 1913. Based on a population of just over five million, this is an extraordinary increase, and one that seemed to be absorbed with equanimity. It would be many decades, and two world wars, before such levels would be achieved again.

In fact, during the First World War and in its aftermath, there was very little immigration. Even through the 1920s the numbers were well less than half those of the booming period in the first dozen years of the century. From about 1930 to 1950, immigration was negligible, reflecting the troubled decades of the Depression and the Second World War.

The Second Surge

The next strong period for immigration began after the Second World War. From about 1950 to 1975, between 100,000 and 150,000 immigrants arrived each year—two-thirds of them from Britain and Europe, and about 10 percent from Asia. In the mid-1980s, that number jumped to about 200,000 per year; and the countries of origin shifted dramatically so that by the end of the twentieth century, less than 20 percent were from Britain, almost half were from Asia, and almost 30 percent were from Africa, the Mideast, and South America. And almost 80 percent of these were visible minorities.

In a sense, the period of the first fifteen years of the twentieth century is similar to 1950–80. The average numbers are about the same, and the countries of origin are Britain and Europe. And in both cases, significant proportions of the immigrants had skills suited to farming and rural pursuits, including the resource-extraction industries. But in the middle of the century, many more of the immigrants went to the cities. Many more of them had skills best suited to urban areas, like brick and tile laying, tool and die making, electrical and mechanical skills, and financial and commercial backgrounds and training.

The dramatic rise in population in our three main cities from 1950 to the present shows this gravitation.

	1950	1980	2000
Toronto	1,250,000	3,000,000	4,650,000
Montreal	1,525,000	2,800,000	3,400,000
Vancouver	575,000	1,250,000	1,950,000

These numbers are remarkable, but not surprising within the worldwide context of urbanization, which is described in another chapter. The combined increase in population of these three cities over fifty years is about 6.7 million people. The population of Canada increased over the same period by about 15 million. These three cities accounted for almost 45 percent of that growth. And Canada accepted about nine million immigrants over that fifty-year span, accounting for 60 percent of all population growth.

The Sifton era and the era since 1985 have two similarities. The average annual numbers are the highest in our history, and about the same. And the nature of the immigrants in both cases was a strong reflection of the country's economy. In Sifton's time, the strength and promise of the economy lay in farming, and his populating of the west led to the development of Canada's wheat industry. For decades, Canada was a world leader not only in growing and trading wheat, but also in wheat science and related crop science and agricultural techniques. Sifton recruited immigrants to move from farms to farms.

At the end of the twentieth century and the start of the twenty-first, the Canadian economy is based on information and design, the underpinnings of the modern world economy. And our immigrants are being admitted based on their suitability to succeed in this new economy. They have high education attainments in their home countries, have experience in the modern economy, and want to work at such jobs in Canada. And, typically, they are coming from cities to cities.

In the period from 1950 to 1985, there were still immigrants who headed to rural Canada, to work in farming and resource extraction. And there were an enormous number who headed into the "old economy," particularly into construction, which along with automobile production was the main driver of the economy for decades after the Second World War.

Peter Flisenberg arrived from Holland in 1952, with his wife, Gerarda, and their four children. They arrived at Pier 21 in Halifax and were immediately transferred to the train waiting at the pier side. These trains, known as "colonist trains," had wooden seats that could be laid flat to make a sleeping platform, but little or no padding. Each car had a wooden stove that, in the winter, would barely be adequate. There are few descriptions of these train trips as anything other than an ordeal, uncomfortable and dispiriting, although there are many comments on the passing scenery. The trains crossed Nova Scotia and New Brunswick into Quebec, and proceeded through Quebec City to Montreal and points west. The Flisenbergs ended up in Woodstock, Ontario, about two hundred kilometres west of Toronto in the heart of southwestern Ontario's farm country. There they were met by the farmer who had sponsored them, and they were put to work on his farm.

A year earlier, Julius Topf had left Hildesheim, Germany, having surveyed the wreckage of his hometown and the general devastation from the war. He had endured a rough crossing, and also found himself on a train, this time heading to the north of the Great Lakes. Topf had wanted to be a veterinarian, but the practical realities of emigration, and the necessity of finding an immediate livelihood, found him in a logging camp near Chapleau, north of Lake Superior, where he learned the arts and labours of felling and limbing pine trees. He lasted a season, then made the move into Sudbury, where he found a job working deep in the ground in the mine shafts of the International Nickel Company.

And the same year, Rudy Alonzi left Sora, in the Lazio region of central Italy, and boarded the ship *Homeric* in Naples to travel to Canada. He was a young child travelling with his family. His father was an ice cream maker, known in Sora as *Il Gelataio*. They travelled from Halifax to Toronto, where they were greeted by an uncle. The father found work in construction and the mother in a factory. There was not a great call in Toronto for gelato makers. Rudy went to school for a few years, and then to work. Eventually he found a job in a brewery, and spent almost three decades there, as he found a wife, had a family, and lived the classic arc of the immigrant life, from initial hardship and privation to an eventual full and comfortable life as a Canadian.*

But if we look ahead twenty-five years to 1975, we are more likely to see Rani Advani, with her bachelor's degree from Bombay University in India, arriving in Canada at age twenty-two with ten dollars, to do her master's degree at the University of Waterloo. After completing her degree, she started National Corporate Name Clearance Corporation, a service to streamline the screening of proposed names for businesses. In 1996 it become OnCorp, providing electronic access to the various programs and services of Ontario's Ministry of Consumer and

---

* Flisenberg, Topf, and Alonzi stories all taken from Pier 21 website, which has a vast collection of immigrant sketches: www.pier21.ca.

Business Services. Ms. Advani built up a successful new-economy business, like a good many of her fellow immigrants from India.

Or we see Lata Pada, born in Bangalore, India, who married a geologist and, after a brief period in Indonesia, ended up in Sudbury, Ontario. Lata was passionate about dance, particularly traditional Indian dance, and spent a part of each year back in India training with the top instructors and gurus. Then, in 1985, she suffered the horrific tragedy of having her husband and two daughters killed in the Air India disaster. She was devastated, but somehow found the strength and courage to carry on, and in 1990 formed the Sampradaya dance company, which combined traditional and modern dance in a way that captured both audiences and critics in India, Canada, and around the world. In the fifteen years since she founded the troupe, it has become world renowned, a great Canadian arts success story, and a great Canadian world product. Many people know Canada through Sampradaya and the creative genius of Lata Pada. This is another great expression of a new-economy triumph.

And for those of us who like our information and design more readily appreciable, there are remarkable chefs who have immigrated to Canada in the late twentieth century, who now grace our cities and towns with innovative and exquisite cooking, in restaurants that are hospitable and comfortable. None characterizes this better than Albino Silva, the proprietor and executive chef of Chiado, a "progressive Portuguese" restaurant in the west end of Toronto's downtown. Silva, an elegant man who grew up in northern Portugal, emigrated to Toronto and began work as a busboy in a restaurant of modest culinary ambitions. He then went to a chain seafood restaurant, becoming a manager, and then spent a year as an instructor at the Culinary Institute of America in New York. Coming back to Toronto, he spent a year as a chef at one of the city's top restaurants before launching

Chiado. At Chiado, he has realized his vision of taking the essential quality of traditional Portuguese cuisine and infusing it with modern technique and high-quality ingredients. He has also been a co-owner of and inspiration to a number of other restaurants in Toronto, but Chiado is his signature, and one of Canada's finest restaurants.

Peter Geary came from England in the late 1970s, after almost a decade of working in high-level hospitality. A tall and graceful man, unsettlingly thin for those of us who bear the baggage of frequent restaurant dining, Geary's sartorial trademark is an apparently endless supply of bright, large bowties, which make it appear as if an extraordinary butterfly is accompanying him on his rounds of welcome and ministration of hospitality. Peter first impressed the Toronto restaurant scene at the front of the house of the Auberge du Pommier, the initial great restaurant of another immigrant, Peter Oliver from South Africa. (Oliver, an extraordinary man, became the country's premier restaurant entrepreneur, teaming up with Welsh immigrant partner Michael Bonacini to create Jump and Canoe, along with a series of other first-class restaurants. Oliver also became renowned for his creation of the Leacock Society, a unique charitable organization that raises money through events that combine wit and social purpose.) Through his work with Oliver, when he became the front-of-house man at Jump, Geary met chef Martin Kuprie, and in 1996 the two of them opened Pangaea, which has become a culinary anchor of Toronto's trendy Bloor Street/Yorkville area.

And there is the remarkable Susur Lee, a late-1970s immigrant from Hong Kong, where he started in the kitchens of that iconic establishment, the Peninsula Hotel. In Toronto he worked in some of the kitchens at the centre of the awakening of food sensibilities in the city. From the great kitchen at the Westbury Hotel, followed by the daringly accessible Peter Pan café on Queen Street West, he gradually began to express his own art, which as it has turned out is an ambitious and generous embrace of the best of many cuisines. From his own Asian roots, the best of European traditions, and whatever else seemed to be superb, Lee has managed to find innovative and satisfying ways to integrate them into something unique. He owns several eponymous restaurants in Toronto, and advises others in Singapore, New York, and elsewhere.

In my hometown of Vancouver, we were aware of the impact of immigrants on the way we ate, and where we did it. Like many businessmen, my father had a number of Chinese- and Japanese-Canadian employees, and we often ate at the restaurants owned by members of their families. At Christmastime we paid ritual visits to their homes and ate the most wonderful food. (Years later, when I owned a business in China, my Chinese hosts would marvel at my skill with chopsticks, unusual for a Westerner, and I told them, "I learned to use them as a kid.") As university students, we found that the best food at the best prices could be found in the Japanese restaurants near the Powell Street Grounds. They also had private dining areas, screened by sliding paper panels, and low tables where you sat cross-legged— all very exotic.

The great immigration boom since the Second World War has broadened and deepened our culinary opportunities so that now, in our largest cities, you can find cuisine from every continent, country, and even county of the world. Within a mile of my home in Toronto, I can go from the heights of Nepal to the flood plain of Bangladesh, from the heat of India to the cool of Japan, and from the olives and tomatoes of the Mediterranean to the caribou of the tundra. And there is Somali food in Ottawa, Moroccan in Winnipeg, Thai in Kamloops, Mexican in St. John's, and Chinese, Indian, and Japanese almost everywhere.

Assets or Liabilities?

Part of the glory of immigration is that it manages itself. Immigrants have a drive to make their lives better, and they prove it by moving halfway around the world to do so. They are incredibly adaptable, self-organizing, and self-reliant. The stories of the people earlier show that. And, typically, the stories of their sons and daughters endorse it further. In fact, they have such a desire to succeed that it takes an extraordinary effort to stand in their way.

Unfortunately, too many countries in the world seem bent on making that extraordinary effort.

In fact, it is often the nations that say they want immigration, and know that they need it for economic reasons, that have the most inexplicable barriers to attracting and retaining immigrants. And there is a reason for this disconnection: we have to decide as societies whether we regard immigration as a good thing, or merely as a problem to be managed. It is a simple choice we can make, but our decision will have a powerful effect on how well we do.

If we view it as good, then we need to see it as an asset in which we invest. It means that we need to clear the way for immigrants and treat them with the respect we show our own citizens. This is something that Clifford Sifton understood, and he cleared the way for the people he attracted to succeed.

If we view immigration as merely a problem to manage, we will tend to think in terms of containing immigrants, of making sure that we limit their impact on society so that they do the least damage. That is, if we let them in at all. It is clearly a very different mindset, and one that is unlikely to work.

So, will we give them wings, or shackles? We can decide.

The Right Immigration Policy

The first thing to do is to make sure we have a good immigration policy. As often as not, like many other policies, what we have is an accumulation of a succession of incremental changes to an original policy. The original policy might have had some cohesion, but the subsequent "fixes" have disintegrated it. So it is always useful to have a view of what a good policy would look like, and there are several elements of a good immigration policy.

It should serve the economy

Immigrants and their new countries are both served when they can fit in quickly economically, creating wealth for themselves and those around them. That works best when they can do the kinds of things for which they have been educated and trained, and in which they have experience. There are too many stories about doctors driving taxis, or technicians sweeping floors, sad examples of our failure to connect immigrants to the economy. We need more effective strategies to link immigrants to the economy quickly, appropriately, and enduringly.

It should build international relationships that serve multiple national objectives

Obviously, immigration can make vital connections between our economy and those of other countries. In 2006, I was at a dinner of the Indo-Canadian Chamber of Commerce, where my colleague Ratna Omidvar was being honoured. Several thousand people were in attendance, including any politician of ambition, and there was a plethora of stories about enormous business successes, not only about immigrants who had succeeded in Canada, but even more impressively about Canadian-based businesses doing massive business in

India. But there are other important relationships that can resound to the benefit of our international goals in peacemaking, peacekeeping, the provision of humanitarian aid, research and education, and arts and culture. It is important to understand that, in Canada, the money immigrants send to their families in their countries of origin is more than five times as much as our international aid budget, and remittances are therefore the lens through which many people will create their view of Canada. These relationships are always at work informally, and the smart country will illuminate and celebrate them.

It should alleviate suffering

The humanitarian component is perhaps the most glorious expression of our immigration policy, not to mention our soul as a people, although this is often the area most fraught with controversy. Canada, like many countries, is a signatory of important international covenants, and we have important domestic precedents that commit us to a code of respect for the individual—such as our Charter of Rights and Freedoms—and judicial precedents that define the nature of our internal relationships. We also have historical practice, such as our support for international development assistance and international diplomacy in pursuit of peace and security, that bind us to the creation of better conditions around the world in order to make people more secure in their home countries. All countries have these bundles of policy, program, and practice that seek humanitarian goals, and we can all enhance them.

It promotes diversity

Diversity is a worthy goal in itself, and it promotes vigour in societies. At a recent Diaspora Dialogues reading in Toronto's Kensington

Market, the Toronto poet Andrea Thompson, reading from the title poem of her CD *One*, said,

> *as a woman of colour*
> *I know—in the future*
> *everyone will look like me*

What a wonderful and encouraging observation that is. We are all familiar with botanical diversity, where smart farmers and gardeners plant a mix of crops for a variety of benefits. They avoid the risks of monoculture, where one germ or insect can wipe out the entire crop. They get the benefit of the natural repellent attributes of one crop keeping the area clear for others. My mother taught me to plant nasturtium flowers around my garden to keep the aphids away from other flowers and plants. It has worked for almost half a century in my garden. That kind of diversity works well in societies, where different ideas, beliefs, and practices can strengthen each other.

This runs very counter to the protectionism prevalent in societies, where we seek to maintain the supposed integrity, if not purity, of our national beliefs and values. As if those beliefs and values themselves were not an amalgam of a multitude of fragments that arrived from different places at different times in our past. The reality of any society is that it is constantly being made and remade by those seeking to make their lives within it. Clearly, we have base-line values that are expressed in our laws; in societies like Canada's, they protect people from violence and harm, but also from discrimination based on race, gender, religion, and other important matters.

■ ■ ■

But it is vital to be clear on one very important thing: how we treat immigrants is absolutely a reflection of how we treat our own citizens. That is, if we are a society with deep class or race divides, we will not settle immigrants well. If we cannot provide the basic services of a modern society—good education, good health care, quality affordable housing, ease of movement, and appropriate access to jobs—to all our own citizens, then we will struggle providing them to immigrants. We will, at best, add to an underclass we already find we aren't prepared to support.

Disconnections: Jobs and Schools

We know for certain that the principal driver of successful immigrant settlement is a good job. A good job is one that fits the skills, training, and ambition of the worker. But too often, immigrants are frustrated on this score, encountering what Naomi Alboim, a former Ontario deputy minister of immigration and a leading commentator on immigration issues, describes as a "broken promise." As she points out, under the rigorous immigrant selection process in place since 1976, Canada proposes to immigrants that it values their skills, education, and language abilities, and that they are being selected on that basis. You get "points" for these things (there is also a family reunification channel, and a refugee channel), and you only have to miss by one point to be denied admission. But then the immigrant discovers in their job search that there are a good many other barriers to the workplace, ranging from professional credentials demanded by non-governmental licensing authorities (bar associations for lawyers, medical associations for doctors, councils for accountants and engineers) to racism, often subtle and subconscious.

The disconnection between the immigration system and the labour market affects more than just immigrants. For example, construction companies complain about the shortage of skilled trades people. One story, perhaps apocryphal, says that the youngest bricklayer in Ottawa is sixty-three years old, and that they can't import bricklayers because you don't get points for bricklaying, and nobody is educating them in Canada. At the same time, in Brazil and Portugal, there are lots of unemployed bricklayers who would love to find work in Canada. And so it goes for sheet-metal workers, tile layers, and tool and die makers.

Governments understand this disconnection, of course, and would like to do something about it. But the Canadian federal government currently has a massive backlog of immigration cases to deal with, and has made that a priority. The backlog, perversely, makes it difficult to change policy because those on the backlog list are there under one set of understandings that may be obviated or violated by any change.

The other great disconnection with the immigration system is the education system. Recent changes to Canadian immigration policy, in 2002, shifted the emphasis slightly towards "human capital." Ideally, bright young immigrants could spend some time attending Canadian colleges and universities, gaining both the skills and insights that would accelerate their successful settlement. But until recently, foreign students didn't qualify for student aid, and attempts to change the law in this regard failed to meet the parliamentary requirement for unanimous approval because the Opposition house leader didn't want to give the governing party a victory. It required parliamentary unanimity because the governing party wouldn't make it a government initiative; thus, it had to move forward as a private member's bill. When the federal government finally made the change, the provinces were slow to implement it, causing delays of several more years, and then many of the individual universities were foot-draggers—mostly, it seems, out of sloth and indolence. So, some bright young woman from Rwanda, looking to remake a life here in Canada, must have stood shocked at this spectre of reluctance, on an issue everyone agreed with substantively.

There is much that the governments can do to make the education system open and welcoming to immigrants. Putting them on the same ground as Canadian students for student aid would be a good start. Supporting programs to ease their adjustment to Canadian ways, perhaps through such able intermediaries as World University Services of Canada, would be helpful. Funding the colleges and universities themselves to develop strong bridging programs, helping the faculties to be more culturally sensitive, and opening up the administrations to new demands, would all serve a useful purpose. Canadian public policy guru Tom Kent has written that this should be at the centre of our immigration policy, an approach that would serve the country and would serve the world. City planning guru Joe Berridge has an equally intriguing idea, one he first voiced when the idea of closing the Toronto Island Airport came up. He said the site should become a new university, an international university that would attract bright and motivated students from every country in the world for an international education based in the modern-economy disciplines of information and design, and they would mix with an equal number of Canadian students drawn from across the country, equally bright and motivated. Toronto's uniquely high diversity (50 percent immigrant, 50 percent visible minority) would make a welcome milieu. In Berridge's mind, half the students might stay after graduation and half go home, and maybe half the Canadians would follow their new friends into the world. Between them, Kent and Berridge have a great vision for Canadian educators.

And while our attention is focused on getting this right, we might look at the connection between the labour market and the education system. How come we don't have enough skilled trades people? Or enough nurses? As the great writer Jane Jacobs used to remind us, everything is connected, and we need to act as if they were, rather than keeping things isolated in their separate silos.

Why Wait for Governments?

But government generally wears too much opprobrium when these issues are discussed. There can be no question that they need to work hard at re-establishing their competency in these areas, but so do the various institutions who have a role in immigrant settlement. Our educational institutions, our employers both public and private, and our community institutions all need to bring themselves to thinking about how they can contribute to make settlement an asset, not just a problem to manage.

And there is much that citizens can do, working together, to help organize better outcomes. For example, much of the work on the issue of recognizing the credentials of foreign-trained professionals has been done by "third-sector" groups. This is a common issue in most developed countries, characterized by the image of the doctor driving the taxi or the engineer delivering pizza. It is critical to separate real issues of competence from those of protecting the market, and to build true bridges that will accelerate the pace at which immigrants find work for which they are trained and capable. Governments have a role to play, but good headway can be made by dealing diligently and respectfully with licensing bodies and trade groups.

As another example, the Maytree Foundation, in conjunction with the Toronto City Summit Alliance, has created the Toronto Region Immigrant Employment Council, or TRIEC, recognizing that the key to successful settlement is finding good work. TRIEC has apprenticeship, mentoring, and learning programs that link immigrants and employers. The key for TRIEC has been to get employers to the table—and they have come in significant numbers, thanks in large part to the leadership of Dominic D'Alessandro and Diane Bean of Manulife Financial, one of Canada's leading companies. Again, government has a role to play, most importantly as major employers, and we're happy to see them coming aboard as supporters of TRIEC. But the initiative has been driven by non-governmental organizations and corporations, each recognizing the economic and social importance of making these vital connections.

Another program that works towards successful long-term settlement is AbcGTA, a program designed to accelerate the participation of immigrants in the plethora of agencies, boards, and commissions (Abc's) in the Greater Toronto Area that govern many aspects of community life. Library, university, college, and hospital boards, community centre boards, public health agencies, and various government agency boards, all play vital community roles, and they should reflect the community in their make-up. Newcomers will feel a stronger attachment to their new country when they see people like themselves in positions of responsibility and authority. AbcGTA has created a list of candidates who are qualified, and it matches them with the vacancies that occur. Many of the agencies, boards, and commissions are keen to become more representative and have been eager to use these services. And AbcGTA is in the process of ongoing outreach.

Diaspora Dialogues is a new program in Toronto, but it has a place in any city in the modern world. It has had two objectives: the first is to let immigrant writers be heard, and to help them find a market for their work; the second is to reflect back to those Canadians who arrived earlier, changing the face of their communities and country. By providing outlets for works that have local Canadian settings and themes, we can see our country anew, and see it differently. We think this will deepen our understanding of who we are and where we live. Cultural expression is a vibrant voice in the democratic marketplace. It is often the place where the most intense, thoughtful, or thrilling voices arise. Through our literature, music, film, painting, and sculpture, we can see a refined depiction of identity, a picture of our country and our communities that reveals useful truths and ideas. Such expressions bubble up in societies, and rapidly in open and democratic environments. But often those marginalized communities need some stimulus to encourage expression. Diaspora Dialogues provides that stimulus.

Another prospective initiative that could enrich the process of settlement is the idea of giving non-citizen residents the ability to vote in municipal elections. This would have numerous benefits. It would allow newcomers to begin acting like citizens right away, and give them a means to influence the set of services and programs they consume. For most citizens, it is municipal services that they encounter most regularly and closely. It would begin to change very quickly the complexion of our elected bodies. And it would infuse local politics with a current dynamism. Toronto's mayor, David Miller, is very attuned to immigrants and their issues, and extending the vote in this way would create a city council supportive of initiatives aimed at more effective settlement. This is a controversial matter, and some have conflated this with participation in federal and provincial elections, which it need not be. It would be an excellent "entry point" to democratic participation for newcomers, many of whom come from countries where elections don't exist. Non-citizens can vote in municipal elections in the Scandinavian countries, as well as in Ireland, Hungary, and the Netherlands, among others. In New Zealand, they can vote in national elections.

There are many reasons to do none of these things: money, politics, incapability, disinterest, and even torpor. But that is to put Canada, or any country, by default into the camp of people who want to manage immigration as a problem, not capitalize on it as an asset. We can choose to hobble people who come to Canada, or empower them. If we do the former, we'll pay a price down the road. If we do the latter, we'll reap benefits.

And immigration isn't going away. In Europe, they've tried closing the doors, and it doesn't work. Even in the UK, with an ocean between it and anywhere else, it doesn't work. It won't work with our oceans and borders, so we had better decide to make the most of it. After all, it has paid us enormous dividends in Canada, as Clifford Sifton and Sir Wilfrid Laurier knew it would.

3

STRONG AND FREE
Twenty-First-Century Challenges with Nineteenth-Century Tools

The dynamic trends of urbanization and immigration have produced a Canada that would barely be recognizable to the Fathers of Confederation. In fact, if a group of Fathers, and Mothers, of Confederation were to gather today at the start of the twenty-first century to design the country, they would come up with something very different.

And the starkest difference would likely be the status of cities. For under the British North America Act of 1867, cities are almost invisible. "Municipal Institutions" is identified as an area of provincial jurisdiction in section 92.8 of the British North America Act, nestled between "Hospitals, Asylums, Charities, and Eleemosynary Institutions" in 92.7 and "Shop, Saloon, Tavern, and Auctioneer" licences in 92.9. The BNA Act effectively allocated responsibilities and authority between the provinces and the federal government. Municipalities were designated as the responsibility of the provinces, with no residual authority of their own. Any authority they were to enjoy would be that permitted by the provincial governments, and could be granted or taken away at the will of the province. Cities, then, had no control of their own destinies.

Control of destiny is the basis on which effective government is built. Without it, governments are unable to deliver to citizens what they expect, what they want, and what they may have been promised. But governments are elected on the basis of having presented a relatively persuasive argument to citizens, some set of indications about what they will do and how they will behave. After the election, citizens wait for these things to happen. Empowered governments can deliver them, or be held accountable for failing. But governments lacking the basic ability to deliver, whose every proposal or action can be overseen or undercut by a "senior" government, cannot be made accountable. They can use their powerlessness as a shield, or as a crutch. This is the plight of cities in Canada, which lack the ability to control their destinies. There are many victims, but perhaps the most serious victim is democracy itself.

In the late 1990s, David Collenette, the Transportation minister in the federal Liberal government of Jean Chrétien, decided that Toronto should have a high-speed rail link between Pearson Airport and Union Station downtown. He began to talk about it with enthusiasm, and he set the wheels in motion to make it happen. Such a project was not on the minds at Toronto city council, or of the city planners, or of the transportation officials at City Hall. They were all having enough trouble keeping existing transit routes running at good service levels, given recent provincial government funding stringency. And other observers thought Collenette's idea was marginal at best, noting that only about 15 percent of Pearson traffic ended up going anywhere near downtown Toronto. If anything was to be done, many of them recommended connecting the Via Rail train system to the airport, which would facilitate travel to the network of southern Ontario cities that uses Pearson as its hub, or the GO Transit system of commuter trains that serve the greater Toronto region. But such views fell on deaf ears, and the project began to plow ahead seemingly inexorably. The only saving grace in the process was the inability of the government to move quickly: a request for proposals was issued in 2000, a request for expressions of interest in 2001, a request for business cases in 2003, a firm selected to build the project in 2005, and a Transport Canada news release issued in 2006. But nothing built.

A similar example is the proposal to build an extension of the Toronto subway to York University in the northwest part of the city. This project has long been a darling of York officials and of politicians from the area, but transportation experts have always thought of it as expensive, unsustainable, and unnecessary. Richard Gilbert, a former Toronto councillor and past president of the Canadian Urban Institute, is an astute transit observer. He notes that the original Toronto subway had the distinction of being the only one in North America that paid for itself almost completely from the fare box, because transportation planning and general development planning went hand in hand. It was city policy to increase density around subway stations. Gilbert says that having 40,000 people living or working within 600 metres of a subway station will make it pay for both its capital and operating costs over a thirty-five-year period. This is medium-density development, with an average of seven storeys, and what Gilbert calls a "generous provision for parks and public spaces." Of course, when you put a new subway line through an existing low-density neighbourhood of single-family homes and low-rise condominiums, you get a NIMBY (Not In My Back Yard) response, so politicians press ahead to provide the desirable amenity (the subway) without the supporting infrastructure (the increased density). They worry about paying for the service later. And which politicians are promoting the York subway? Is it the mayor of Toronto, or the Toronto city council? No: according to a report in the December 8, 2006, *Toronto Star* it is federal Finance minister Jim Flaherty, who hails from Whitby, east of Toronto, and then Ontario Finance minister Greg Sorbara, whose riding abuts York University. The federal and provincial governments may or may not provide some of the capital costs of the new line, but there is no mention of ongoing support for the operating costs. Those responsibilities would fall to the mayor and council of Toronto, but this isn't really their decision.

These kinds of separations of responsibility and accountability are highly problematic. In both these cases, politicians from other levels of government have an enormous influence over the future of a city. In each case, an expensive piece of infrastructure would be put in place that would alter land use and transportation patterns, without being integrated with the overall plan of the city. In fact, the plan would have to be changed to accommodate the new rail line. In each case, there is a reasonable constituency of support for the rail line, and thus it can be argued that it is not a total imposition. But federal and provincial politicians are not elected to run the city. Municipal politicians are, and voters expect to be able to hold them accountable. But if one of those lines gets built, like the white elephant Sheppard Avenue subway line before them, voters angry at the high capital costs and ongoing operating deficits will go to their municipal council to complain and will be met with the suggestion that they go talk to Collenette, Flaherty, or Sorbara—who, in the unlikely event they are still holding public office, will say that it is a municipal concern and they should talk to their city councillor.

This lack of control of destiny has a number of dimensions. First, there is a lack of fiscal control. Provincial governments control the fiscal revenue tools available to cities, and generally let the expenditure obligations pile up, particularly as cities get bigger, more complex, and experience more demands. In some cases they actively download additional responsibilities onto cities. The result is annual budgetary deficits in most large Canadian cities, which must then ask provincial governments to help resolve them. Second, there are deficient powers in city governments, as provinces reserve the right to dictate what is allowed and what is not. Many of the things that are critically important to city dwellers, and which affect the quality of urban life, are not under the control of their city government. For example, many city residents are upset by the presence of homeless people on their streets, people who often have serious psychiatric problems. But it is not within the ability of most city governments to construct the assisted housing that could house and help these people. Third, there is insufficient control over the governance structures by cities, so they cannot tailor their government infrastructure to meet their challenges. Cities cannot even decide on the sizes of their own councils or the length of time between elections, and in some cases elected officials and councils have been dismissed by provincial governments and forced to run under new circumstances, as in Toronto in 1997.

The situation is not sustainable at a time in history where competitive city regions are the keys to national success. Cities need to have the capacity to outfit themselves to succeed. They need to be able to put in place the infrastructure required, things like airports, commuter transit systems, wireless communication networks, and utilities for the effective operation of the buildings where people live and work. They must be able to develop an environment that can attract the required labour force, as University of Toronto economist Richard Florida has pointed out in his book The Creative Class. Knowledge workers will go to places that offer not just good jobs, but social and cultural amenities like theatres, parks, restaurants, and dance clubs. Cities must be able to set the regulatory environment to encourage such things. And they must be able to establish the human capital infrastructure in the form of a great school system, world-class universities and colleges, and leading hospitals. They must be able to do all these things without asking permission, without looking over their shoulders, and without fear of having something granted and then withdrawn. Without that sense of capability, cities will typically flinch and underplay their already meagre hands.

Of course, many have argued, all it takes is some real leadership, a mayor with lots of gusto who can make friends and influence people, and make political or financial barriers disappear. We just need stronger mayors, they claim. But there is a problem with a political system that demands heroics to produce success. While heroics are always wonderful to contemplate, and even better to see in action, they aren't always readily available. Political systems are more functional when all you need is good people winning public office and exercising their responsibilities to their fellow citizens.

The fact that in Canada we have not had a steady supply of heroes occupying mayor's offices has led a number of people to the conclusion that we need a "New Deal for Cities." People like economist David Nowlan or public servant Don Stevenson have been saying this for decades. In recent years the subject has again come onto the public agenda, prompted by people like Jane Jacobs. She had Paul Martin over for tea one day, when he was federal Finance minister. He subsequently began to talk about the importance of cities, and when he became prime minister he elevated the pitch of his rhetoric. And the *Toronto Star* began to tout its "New Deal for Cities," which began as a year-long campaign for the newspaper and has since become one of its standards. Many others have joined in the chorus, but the music they sing is anything but harmonious. Listening to it all, one could be forgiven for not quite understanding what the New Deal is.

The Old Deal for Cities

Well, if there is to be a New Deal, there must have been an Old Deal, and it might help to understand what that was.

In fact, there was an old deal, but under it there were good days and bad days.

The good days were those when the federal and provincial governments looked sympathetically and kindly upon cities. As it happened, the fiscal situation at both those levels of government was flush, and they had no problem sending city governments money for transit, housing, social programs, settlement of immigrants, and infrastructure of various sorts. This was during the time of the federal government of Pierre Trudeau, which established a ministry of state for urban affairs. It didn't last all that long, victim in part of provincial jealousy about federal incursion into section 92.8 of the BNA Act. But it was intended to be the friend of the cities. In Ontario, the government of William Davis was happy to help out the cities. In fact, it was even willing to bend to the will of the cities, as it did when it cancelled the Spadina Expressway, which was poised to pierce the heart of a series of old neighbourhoods on its way downtown and which had been the object of vigorous opposition on the part of citizens—including Jane Jacobs.

In fact, in many cities across the country during the 1960s and '70s—and into the '80s—the good times rolled. Transit systems were built and expanded, waterfronts were reclaimed from industrial use or dereliction and turned into neighbourhoods or playgrounds, downtowns were repaved and landscaped, festivals and games were mounted and supported, and stadia, concert halls, museums, and rinks arose. Happy-faced politicians cut ribbons—mayors, premiers, and prime ministers so happy together. Those were the days, the good days, under the old deal for cities.

And they were so good because the country was flush—or at least was under the impression it was. If something was worthwhile, it was done. The federal government spent. The provinces spent. And the cities were the happy beneficiaries of much of this spending. Mayors found it relatively easy to find a funding partner for their projects, and everyone was happy to share credit at the ribbon-cutting.

There were also bad days under the old deal for cities, and they tended to come after the unhappy discovery that the country was not as flush as we thought. Although the national accounts showed it earlier, it was the steep recession of the early 1990s that brought the news home. The bilious laments of groups like the Fraser Institute warned that Canada had become a "banana republic," mired in debt and doomed to collapse. There began a toxic chain of "downloading," as it became known—the process whereby the federal government stopped doing things but kept the revenue that paid for it, a gambit that was copied by the provinces, which assigned obligations to the cities but not the money to pay for them. For some reason, this technique had not been discovered by the federal Conservative government of Brian Mulroney, but Jean Chrétien and his finance minister Paul Martin found it, and played it for all it was worth. Another happy practitioner was Ontario premier Mike Harris, who seemed to embrace the practice with some relish, and no slight malice.

So, in the bad days under the old deal, the federal government was obsessed with fixing the federal accounts by reducing the annual deficits and paying down the national debt. They achieved their objectives by downloading, cutting program spending, and hiding as much revenue as they possibly could. They were undeterred by reports of suffering coming up from the coal face of poverty and need. They were undeterred even by the rising economy, which could have allowed a judicious mix of deficit slaying, debt reduction, and program spending, enough to bring Canada's debt-to-GDP ratio to the lowest in the G8 within ten years (according to a study done by Michael Mendelson at the Caledon Institute, which proved to be true).

Chrétien didn't have time for the cities. They were the responsibility of the provinces—end of story. His neglect was as majestic as he could muster—a wave of the hand, a quip, and long strides off into the distance. Martin seemed to think differently—which annoyed Chrétien, by all accounts—but he did little until his own moment in the spotlight after Chrétien was forced out.

In fact, to give Martin some credit, he managed to recreate a good afternoon, if not a good day, when he said that proceeds from a part of the federal tax on gasoline would go to the cities—a sum of money that turned out to be welcome but not material for most cities.

Nowhere were the bad days worse than in Ontario, and in the Toronto region in particular. Mike Harris not only had budget problems of his own, but he didn't like Toronto. He felt it was the home to all sorts of people who didn't like him and his government, and he seemingly set out to prove it. A churlish fellow anyway, Toronto's self-regarding ways seemed to set him off. There were any number of slights and deprivations that he was happy to foist on the city, but the true measure of hostility was his dismissal of Toronto's mayor and council, along with those of the other cities that made up Metropolitan Toronto (Scarborough, York, North York, East York, and Etobicoke), and their forced amalgamation into the new city of Toronto. Citizens were outraged, and organized a citizen-driven referendum that attracted a high voter turnout and rejected amalgamation by huge majorities. The province chose not to recognize the referendum, and proceeded anyway. The ill will and resistance doomed the smooth implementation of amalgamation, and a decade later neither the politics nor the administration of the new city have matured. Harris seemed unmoved, and the hostility that characterized his approach to the city eventually came around and forced him from office in the face of declining respect for him and appetite for his party.

Other provinces downloaded to fix their budgets, too, notably British Columbia, but it was generally done with better feeling than in Ontario. There wasn't the hostility. Mind you, the cities didn't embrace it, but they bore it.

Under the old deal for cities, there were good and bad days, and the thing they had in common was that the cities had no control of their destinies. Good day or bad, someone else made the decisions. Even when Martin decided to send along some of the gas tax money, the cities had to submit plans to the federal government to qualify, and they had to fit a template based on environmental sustainability that the feds had developed. This was just a different version of the Collenette rail line to the airport or the Flaherty subway to York University.

Those decisions may have been made with a view towards helping cities, or with a view to punishing them, or without them in view at all, but the decisions were made somewhere other than in the office of a mayor or on the floor of a city council chamber. And it happened this way because the purse strings, the actual ability to pay for and implement policy and programs, were held elsewhere. Cities relied on the kindness of strangers, which was in sporadic supply.

The New Deal: Control of Destiny

Control of destiny is at the heart of the new deal for cities. Cities need to be able to have a vision of their future, to create a credible plan to get there, and to implement the policies and programs that make that future vision a reality. If there is a disconnection in that effective chain, cities will founder.

One of the outcomes of such disconnections is that the behaviour of city governments begins to disintegrate. When a councillor knows that she does not have the powers or money to deliver something, and can demonstrate her incapacity, she might be prone to making the promise anyway and pointing the finger at another level of government when the time comes to account. In effect, the practice of provincial and federal governments treating city governments like children tends to make them act like children. And anyone who has raised children knows that they become responsible people by being given responsibility.

There is an interesting example of exactly this phenomenon in Ontario, which has a unique body called the Ontario Municipal Board (OMB). The OMB was created in 1897 to regulate land use and planning decisions made by municipalities. Over the years, it has become the place of final appeal of decisions made by municipal governments, so if a citizen or developer doesn't like the official response to an application they have made, they can ask the OMB to reconsider it. The only appeal beyond the OMB is to the provincial government of the day, which rarely overturns an OMB decision. Members of the OMB are appointed by the Ontario government and serve in a quasi-judicial fashion, hearing evidence on the cases before them and rendering verdicts.

In practice, the OMB has disempowered city planning departments. For example, in 2006, in an area of Toronto known as the Queen West Triangle, which had developed a bohemian quality because of the artists who were living and working in the older industrial and commercial buildings, a group of property developers proposed to level the old buildings and put up a massive amount of condominiums. The proposed new development would consist of high-rise studio, one- and two-bedroom apartments. When local residents and business owners got wind of what was happening, they put together a group of planners, architects, and lawyers to come up with an alternate plan that would give developers most of what they wanted, but would preserve space for artists and would have three- and four-bedroom units to accommodate families. They took these plans to City Hall and got the endorsement of the mayor and the planning department. But rather than becoming actively engaged, both the mayor and planners did almost nothing, either for the neighbourhood or the developers. When the six-month approval deadline passed without the city rendering a decision, the developers took their original proposals to the OMB, which rendered approval several months later. All of the effort at compromise by the neighbourhood went for naught. When asked subsequently what had gone wrong, a senior official in the planning department said, "I guess we fell behind the curve." No kidding.

In all probability, the planning department anticipated that any decision they might have rendered other than outright approval of the developers' plans would have been referred to the OMB anyway, so they felt no urgency in getting down to work. Nor did they seem to feel any obligation to a group of citizens who had worked hard at developing a compromise. The OMB is an all-or-nothing body, and it tends to give thumbs up or down on proposals. And for most of its history it has tended to support developers and big development, without much concern over issues like design, quality, or neighbourhood impact. And city planners have learned to flinch appropriately, relinquishing their own sense of vision, design, quality, impact, and integration with their own official plans. They know that the power lies elsewhere on these matters, and that there is enough money at stake to ensure that developers will seek the court of last appeal. The effect is disastrous. As an internationally renowned architect and planner, Ken Greenberg, said after the OMB decision: "If there's anything to be learned, it's that we have a truly dysfunctional planning system in this city. And a lot of that has to do with the OMB."

The OMB is a relic of the old deal for cities, and a classic example of what needs to change if a truly new deal is to occur. Developers will say, quite rightly, that any development approvals process needs an appeal process. Builders need some defence against decisions that may be made on purely political grounds, and against power exercised in an unfair or unclear way. But there is no reason why such an appeal process needs to be located at another level of government. It could as easily be a city process, with appropriate structural and procedural safeguards to isolate it from the same people and influences that rendered the decision being appealed. This is how it is done in almost every other jurisdiction in the world, many of them absolutely analogous to Ontario cities. It is the way it is done in other parts of Canada.

What fundamentally separates the new deal from the old is the question of control of destiny. Under the old deal, authority and accountability were divided. Citizens of the city elected their councillors and expected them to be able to deliver on a wide range of issues affecting the city, from trash collection to good roads to public health to services for the homeless. But ultimately all of those things could be dramatically affected by the action of a provincial government or the federal government, either intentionally or unintentionally. It is uncertain whether Paul Martin actually anticipated the consequences for cities of his downloading of obligations to provinces in the mid-1990s as he tried to fix the federal budget deficit. It is ironic that he subsequently cast himself as the saviour of cities with his efforts during his short tenure as prime minister, efforts that sent a trickle of money to the city relative to the costs that had been downloaded by provinces in the chain reaction that Martin started.

To Tax Is to Govern

The true mark of the new deal will be the joining of authority and accountability, and to make that happen cities must be given the ability to raise sufficient revenues to afford the future they envision. The question of finance warrants a separate chapter later in this book. It is the fundamental basis of effective government. In effect, to tax is to govern. Without an independent and adequate ability to raise the money to pay for the things that the city needs and wants, a government can never meet the expectations of its citizens.

Canadian cities are particularly handcuffed fiscally. They all rely very heavily on property tax. Canadian cities get about 50 percent of their revenues from property tax, while in the US it is about 15 percent and in Europe it is about 5 percent. In the US and Europe, cities have access to a much broader array of revenue tools, including income tax and taxes on consumption, such as sales tax, hotel tax, liquor tax, and gasoline tax. The problem with property tax is that it doesn't grow apace with the economy. Property values change slowly. When the economy does well, income taxes and sales taxes rise accordingly. Those taxes also get levied on everyone who earns or buys, whereas property tax only is levied on residents. People from outside the city— tourists and commuters—effectively get a free ride when they use taxpayer-provided services and infrastructure.

The other half of the revenues of Canadian cities come from a variety of fees for things like development or licences for commercial operations (over 30 percent), and conditional grants from the provincial and federal governments (less than 20 percent). Some, like the fees, are under their control, although provinces generally set limits on the nature and level.

The new deal would recognize this vital requirement of secure revenue sources for cities, and would empower cities to levy a full range of taxes and to have access to a full range of debt instruments as well. As will be discussed later, this would permit a city to adopt a mix of revenue and debt instruments appropriate to its needs, scale, capacity to manage, and political appetite. It is only when a government has confidence about how much is has to spend that it can begin to plan effectively, knowing that it will have the capacity to do what it decides to do. It can plan its transit system, its waste management system, its parks and arenas, its new housing and commercial development, in confidence that the rug won't be pulled out from beneath the plan.

Anything that looks like a grant from another level of government, or that can be withdrawn unilaterally, or is only available depending on criteria set by another government, is part of the old deal. Any instrument or program that can be unilaterally withdrawn is part of the old deal. There will often be arrangements that rely on agreement and cooperation between two governments, but the partners must have equal status and equal rights at the table. No one should have a trump card. Jurisdictional and constitutional trump cards are part of the old deal.

A real new deal would allow cities to levy the full range of taxes, if they chose to. It would allow cities to issue debt, float bonds, and use other debt-like instruments. Cities around the world are experimenting with new financial tools, looking for the most appropriate ones for the particular jobs at hand. Canadian cities are much less likely to engage in such experimentation because of their fear of interference from their provincial or federal counterparts. In fact, one of the criticisms many have of Canadian municipalities is their timidity, their reluctance to fully use even those tools that are available to them. Again, they have been treated like children for so long that they have adopted childlike reluctance.

There is a very good argument to be made that the federal and provincial governments should be involved in funding cities directly. It is often noted that Canada is alone among the developed nations in not having a national program for funding urban transit or low-income and assisted housing. Canada's federal government used to fund these things, but let them become victims of tight budgets in the 1980s and '90s. And certainly the cities would welcome the resumption of such funding. But if it came with strings attached, if the basic decisions were being made by the federal government, it would certainly not count as a component of a "new deal." And it would not be optimal. It would be less likely to align with existing city plans at the outset, and when the time came to alter plans, as life in the real world usually requires, it would be cumbersome—and perhaps futile—to go back to the funder and seek agreement. Funding from the federal or provincial governments that was guaranteed over a long period of time and came as a block grant without a lot of terms and conditions attached—other than that it be used generally for housing or transit— would be a way to get around this. This is the kind of funding that is transferred for universities or health care. Recent federal governments have become reluctant to make these kinds of grants, because some of the provinces have interpreted rather liberally what they might be applied to, sometimes treating them like general revenues to be allocated to local priorities. Thus the tendency of the Stephen Harper government to apply a strict fiscal interpretation of the federation, under which the provinces would raise money through their own tax mechanisms for their own responsibilities. Extending this to the cities, or at least to the large metropolitan regions, would allow for the joining of authority and accountability that leads to greater control of destiny.

City Powers Must Be Strengthened

Along with independent new fiscal powers to raise revenues, cities also need legislative powers to control their destinies. Historically, Canadian cities have operated within a prescriptive set of powers. The provinces have listed the things that cities are permitted to do, and they must seek permission for anything else they want to do. In some cases the permission is granted expeditiously, but as often as not there are bureaucratic or political delays that can mitigate a city's ability to act in a timely way. In recent years, a number of provinces have moved towards a more permissive system, under which they would effectively define what cities could not do, assuming that the cities would then be able to do anything else. In Ontario, the revisions to the Ontario Municipal Act and the City of Toronto Act have moved in this direction by saying that where a provincial interest exists, the province retains authority, but that the onus rests on the province to show its interest. If Ontario does not claim a provincial interest, or cannot show it, the city has the right to act.

There is a lively discussion about what constitutes appropriate powers for cities. It depends very much on the size and complexity of a city. Some would argue that a city like Toronto should essentially have the powers of a province, including control over its education and health care systems, and this will be discussed in another chapter. But such powers would not make sense for Kapuskasing or Kelowna, which are of a very different size and complexity. Smaller centres may not have a robust tax base, nor the complexity in the local economy that provides for resilience when one sector of the economy is suffering. Many cities may not want many additional powers, preferring instead to rely on another level of government and on being part of a larger pool that would have advantages of scale in the provision of services and programs and might provide some insurance in the case of a localized downturn or problem. For example, many towns and cities don't want to have their own police forces, so they rely on the Royal Canadian Mounted Police or a provincial police force like the Sûreté du Québec or the Ontario Provincial Police.

A new deal for cities would give them a voice in defining the powers they want. A city like Montreal or Vancouver might choose a robust set of powers. They would, of course, recognize the responsibilities that attend the powers and be prepared to organize themselves to shoulder those responsibilities. The toughest one for the big cities would be levying local taxes, because nobody wants to be seen as the tax increaser. It would have to be a secure city government at the start of a long term of office. It looks like political suicide. Even if it is done in the context of stepping in to assume tax space the province or federal government has vacated—say, by a drop in sales or income tax—it would appear to be taking away a benefit another government granted. We seldom see that kind of bravery in politics these days. As premier of Ontario, Dalton McGuinty imposed a new health care tax at the start of his first term in office; he called it a health care premium for a while, until that term became a bit worn out and he admitted it was a tax increase. To his credit, he then made the argument about why it was necessary, and wore it bravely, despite ongoing opposition savaging of him and his "premium."

We are a long way from giving Canadian cities more control of their destinies. There may be more money forthcoming from Ottawa and the provinces, but it will be a repeat of good days under the old deal for cities. To tax is to govern; to spend tax dollars is to exercise power. Power holds immense allure for politicians. The idea that someone else might have better ideas on how to spend fades alarmingly quickly from the minds of even the most sensible of politicians. Even the tremendously sensible and bright John Godfrey, Paul Martin's minister of state for infrastructure and communities, became highly prescriptive when his ministry began to distribute some gasoline tax dollars to cities and communities, setting quite defined criteria under which they qualified for the money, based around principles of environmental sustainability. Environmental sustainability is a good idea, most would agree, but so is trusting local communities to be able to define their own priorities and develop their own projects.

The new deal for cities lacks any common agreement on what would actually constitute it. It would be useful to have some definition of the fiscal tools that might fund it, the powers that might drive it, and the governance structure that might organize it.

4

SONS COMMAND
Control of Destiny for Our Cities

Along a block of Bloor Street outside my office in Toronto there are a number of street people who have been there for the better part of a decade. There is Norm, a gentle giant of a man who has been on disability from a truck driving accident. Norm has a place to live, picks up a little pocket money with a hat held mildly in front of him, and keeps steady hours. One day a few years ago, Norm told me he was turning sixty-four the next day, and that a year hence he was going to retire, which pretty well summed up Norm's sense of obligation to show up. He knows all the regulars along the street. He knows who has arrived, who must be sick because they haven't been along for a few days, and who is coming and going from the various buildings. Back in the first years I had my office on Norm's turf, I was coming into the office one morning just before 10:00 a.m. Norm saw me coming, and when I approached his post he said, with a touch of the scold in his voice, "Well, look who's keeping banker's hours."

Larry (not his real name) is there for a few months or years, then disappears for months at a time, and then comes back. He is a bit high-strung. He's absent when he finds a job, and he returns when his volatility has got him fired. Then there is Ivan (not his real name), who slouches in front of McDonald's and gets steadily obliterated by some substance as the evening turns to night. From time to time, but quite regularly, a group of three Aboriginal men roam the block in a state of inebriation, not causing much trouble, but scaring passers-by with their highly dishevelled appearance and their loud demeanour. Larry and Ivan would probably benefit from some regular psychological and medical assistance to even out Larry's volatility and deal with Ivan's disease of addiction. The Aboriginal men have a more severe abuse problem and could really use some help.

During a typical year, I travel regularly to an office on Cambie Street in Vancouver's Gastown, but not frequently enough to know the names of the men and one woman I see on the street there. But I suspect that they, like my Toronto street mates, would benefit from some regular help, perhaps delivered through assisted housing. And in Montreal, I see similar people along St. Catherine Street, or on Victoria's Government Street near Bastion Square. In any city in our country, you can see these people who would benefit from some assistance, who might not be on the street begging if they got it. Some, like Norm, are there because it is their "office," where they meet people and have a function. But a lot don't really want to be there, and aren't being helped by being there.

Many of our street people are former psychiatric patients, sent out onto the streets when it was decided that keeping them in institutions was a bad idea. It was probably a bad idea to keep them in the large mental hospitals of the day, which were carry-overs from the insane asylums of the nineteenth and first half of the twentieth centuries. But we didn't really replace them with anything, and the patients ended up in unsupervised rooming houses where those with more extreme behaviour got evicted.

Specialists in homelessness know there is a compelling answer that can help a very high percentage of our street people: assisted housing, which is accommodation where there is supervision by on-site social or paramedical workers who can provide practical help and can monitor behaviour and medication. It is a tremendously powerful intervention for health, and also cost-effective because it prevents people from falling into extremes where they end up in the really costly places: hospitals and jails.

In a 2006 *New Yorker* article called "Million-Dollar Murray," Malcolm Gladwell followed a Reno, Nevada, street person who had severe alcohol disease, which caused him to end up several times a year in hospital, where he required major interventions to keep him from dying or becoming seriously compromised by organ damage. He was always harmless, not given to violence or crime, and was well liked by police, medical workers, and the social workers who tried to deal with him. Gladwell calculated that Murray cost the public purse about $100,000 per year in hospital medical costs alone, and if you added in all the policing, ambulance, and social work costs, it would be much more. On a few occasions, Murray had been placed in a program where he had been supervised, given a job and a place to live, and he had done well. He was a good worker and was able to save some money. But when the program ended, and the supervision evaporated, Murray would hit the streets and the bottle and drink up everything he'd saved. Then he'd be back in hospital or jail, and back using expensive public resources. Any expert would say that it was a lot cheaper to rent Murray a studio apartment in a building with a social work supervisor who could make sure he went to work and stayed dry.

Such solutions don't work for every street person, because some people are so sick emotionally or physically that they can't be easily helped. But people like Bob Hohler of the Melville Charitable Trust in New England, which specializes in homelessness, say that assisted housing is as close to a silver bullet as there is in the field, and he has built a national network in the US to create as much of it as possible.

People in Vancouver, Edmonton, Regina, Hamilton, Trois-Rivières, or Moncton know the same thing. And in most of those cities, someone at some time in the last couple of decades has looked at the homeless and proposed building assisted housing to get them off the street and into care.

For a city to do so requires the participation of another level of government, because of the amount of funding required. Or the city has to undertake its own financing scheme, which might involve borrowing or issuing debt that could be serviced from per-diem provincial funding support for the people who would go into care. But here they would run up against their lack of powers to innovate solutions.

Many Canadian cities are prohibited by their provinces from going into debt. Others have severe limits on what taxes they can levy, including restrictions on the scope and rate of such taxes, and on what other financial tools they can use. Even where cities are permitted to assume some debt, the province often describes what kind of debt and to what level. Worse, these conditions can and do change from time to time, often without warning or consultation.

Such unpredictability and limitations make it risky to mount a municipal assisted-housing project that would require long-term financing with some assurance of funding sources for meeting debt obligations. It would be disastrous, for example, to undertake a significant debt to build a project based on, say, a property tax surcharge and the use of provincial disability payments to tenants that might be applied in part against the debt, only to have the province disallow the tax surcharge or put a restriction on the use of the disability payments. Long-term financing requires stable conditions, but cities lack the powers to guarantee those conditions.

There are critics of city governments who say they don't use the tools that are available to them, and that is an accurate observation. Cities have definitely become gun-shy, some even shell-shocked.

There is also a tremendous problem of overlapping jurisdictions. Some of the biggest property owners in Canadian cities are the federal and provincial governments. They own "Crown lands" in cities, often through bodies that control ports, airports, and railway corridors. So, often the large areas of land that are identified as candidates for renewal may have many owners, including federal, provincial, and municipal governments and many private owners.

Vancouver's Expo 86 Bid: Province Trumps City

In the late 1970s, Sam Bawlf and some other members of the British Columbia Legislature looked ahead to Vancouver's centenary in 1986 and thought it should be celebrated with an international exposition, which ultimately became known as Expo 86. Bawlf represented a Vancouver riding. There were several possible sites: the Pacific National Exhibition grounds in the east end of the city; the Coal Harbour area near the heart of downtown, in the vicinity of the historic Canadian Pacific Railway station; and an area a few miles south, on the north shore of False Creek, a former industrial area that was mostly abandoned and derelict. Each had its advocates. The PNE people saw an expo as an ideal way to upgrade their buildings and facilities, but after scoping out what was required, the site was found to be too small. That left the two sites closer to the centre of the city.

City council had a clear point of view: it preferred the site on the harbour. It was close to most of the downtown attractions and to the existing transportation infrastructure, such as it was in Vancouver (whose geography mitigates against an efficient public transit system, and whose politicians have not done much better). More critically, they saw it as a way to clean up and vitalize a key area of downtown, tying together the Gastown tourist area and Stanley Park, one of the world's great urban parks, with a dynamic urban strip along the sea front. There was not a great deal of land available on the site, but it was thought that some landfill could provide sufficient acreage.

Proponents of the False Creek site pointed out that there was plenty of land available, and that the expo development would, over time, flow nicely into the development on the south shore of False Creek, where residential buildings and a sea walk continued agreeably into Granville Island, the public market and artistic precinct that had recently sprouted in the shadow of the Granville Street Bridge. There were also some very practical considerations. The city was trying to buy the lands from the CPR, which was letting them lie underutilized, and the money and energy that would accompany development would spur renewal of the area. There was also the hope that it would have a significant spillover effect into the old warehouse district directly to the north, which would ultimately become the thriving Yaletown.

What ensued in the late 1970s and early '80s was a battle of wills and interests between levels of government and the various private owners at both sites. In 1980, the Bureau of International Expositions approved the Vancouver submission and suggested the False Creek site as the easier and more likely of the two. Then began a real tussle over who would pay for what, who had the most authority, and what would actually occur on the ground. It got so difficult that in 1981, five years before the expo was to open, the British Columbia government suddenly cancelled it. In effect, it told the city it couldn't do it, and let the federal government know that it was over.

Subsequently, cooler heads wary of national embarrassment prevailed. The fair was revived, and in 1986 Vancouver was host to a successful expo that transformed the False Creek area and Yaletown as well. But the instructive moment for city watchers was the unilateral power of the province to take away a powerful city-building opportunity for Vancouver, and to put it back on the table. The other instructive moment was the inability of the city council to control the destiny of its city, to have the expo on the site it preferred, which in its view was in alignment with the official plan for the growth of the city. These things were clearly in the hands of other levels of government that had the powers, and the finances, to make them happen—or not.

Such a story may not have impressed others across the country at the time, but people living in Toronto have come to relate to it. A similar, if more pathetic, story is unfolding along Toronto's waterfront. That strip of waterfront from the Canadian National Exhibition grounds and Ontario Place six miles east to the Beach neighbourhood is a motley array of old industrial and utility buildings, spotty residential and commercial towers, parkland, derelict industrial sites either abandoned or in ruins, and land going roughly back to nature. None of it has the grace or unified appearance of Vancouver's Coal Harbour and False Creek areas, Halifax's waterfront, or Montreal's riverfront. To boot, there is an active, small airport on the most westerly of the offshore Toronto Islands, the wonderful parkland and residential archipelago a ten-minute ferry ride from downtown. The airport occupies prime real estate, runs low-volume traffic, and stands as a barrier to the successful creation of dynamic neighbourhoods on Lake Ontario that could beautifully absorb a significant number of the additional million residents Toronto expects in the next few decades.

But the progress of waterfront development has been stymied by differences between the federal, provincial, and municipal governments and their agencies. A federal agency, the Toronto Port Authority, which controls several sites including the airport, has been so uncooperative that it has even sued the city. The federal member of Parliament with designated responsibility for Toronto in the Martin government, Joe Volpe, was widely rumoured to be opposed to any progress while David Miller was mayor. The reason was that Miller had had the temerity during a federal election to support a candidate who was not a Liberal party member, although the candidate in question had long been an effective city council colleague of Miller's. Provincial support came and went—absent depending on the current whim of the Mike Harris government in the 1990s, more present with the subsequent McGuinty government, which seems to see waterfront development as a critical asset for Toronto and the province.

Again, as in the Vancouver story, the views of city council don't count for a lot, nor do the views of the mayor's office. They are but one voice in the mix, and not the most powerful voice. In fact, in Toronto the disempowerment has become so entrenched that council seems dissociated from the issues. In the summer of 2007, council voted to defer a vote on two much-needed taxes in the fanciful hope that the rival parties would outdo one another in the upcoming provincial election in promising to send Toronto enough money to obviate the need for the taxes. During the election there was no such debate, and none of the dissenting councillors bothered to raise their voices. These councillors clearly don't venture outside the city enough to see how "more money for Toronto" would play with other Ontarians.

Cities Lack Necessary Powers

The lack of powers for Canadian cities is finally becoming so apparent that it is stimulating a process of change. Lawyer Ron Kanter, a former Toronto alderman and member of the provincial Parliament, has written about the limits of those powers: an inability to establish road tolls; an inability to charge for the use of telecommunication lines except at levels that merely recover the costs of issuing the permits; no ability to create public-private partnerships to operate transit or many other utilities; and no ability to negotiate density "bonusing" with developers as a means of realizing planning objectives. And almost no innovative revenue tools, such as the ability to borrow against anticipated tax revenue increases due to improvements to an area, are allowed.

The traditional approach to this lack of power has been incremental. A city would identify a particular grant or instrument it needed and seek to get it from the provincial government, or occasionally the federal government. Often it worked, and the fact that our cities have been able to make progress is a testament to that. Former Toronto mayor David Crombie has made the argument that incrementalism works, and that voters need to elect mayors who can make it work. It has the advantage of making sure that the powers cities get are really needed and have very practical applications. And it avoids yet another generalized reshuffling of duties that may work for the moment in present conditions, but less well at a later date when economics and politics might be quite different. This view presumes that politics is a hands-on practice that plays out practically on the ground and gives itself uncomfortably to grand designs.

A somewhat more ambitious approach might be to seek broader powers from a provincial government, to identify some key levers the city needs to control for better city building. This might be achieved through a specific identification of those areas of greater control, or through a shift in the nature of the legislative relationship from prescriptive to permissive. That is, instead of the province prescribing what a city could do and requiring it to seek approval for everything else, it would describe what a city could not do—presumably those things with a direct provincial interest—and give it permission to do everything else.

During the renegotiation of the City of Toronto Act in 2004–05, there was an interesting dance between the city and the province. The city's first approach was to construct a list of all the powers it felt it needed. It asked all its departments to consider in great detail all of the things it did that had any interface with the province and decide what would be useful to include on the list. When the staff in Municipal Affairs minister John Gerretsen's office got wind of this, they were aghast. In their view, there was an enormous opportunity to recast the relationship from a prescriptive to a permissive one. In the ministry's view, the city should ask for broad powers and require the province to spell out areas of specific provincial interest where control must be retained at Queen's Park. Once the city understood this, it shifted its view and began to think more along those lines. It still carried on with a detailed review of all the legislation that existed on many fronts between the city and province, but were more prepared to take a macro view. But then the province's position got more complicated, as other ministries got involved and began to take a more micro view, several of them thinking in terms of the power they stood to lose rather than ways of fixing a situation that was limiting the cities. Once this happened, the city began to feel betrayed, as if it were being led down the garden path, and the province started to feel that the city was unpredictable. A number of intermediaries began discussions with the offices of the premier, mayor, and city chief administrative officer, and finally the situation calmed down. The new City of Toronto Act that was passed represents a compromise between the prescriptive and permissive approaches, albeit one that does shift the onus onto the province to show the provincial interest in areas of disputed jurisdiction.

When the Act passed, a number of critics balked at it, particularly those sections that strengthened the role of the mayor. Former Toronto mayors David Crombie and John Sewell objected. Crombie thought it gave mayors too much power, which, from his experience, they didn't need. We don't need a strong mayor system, he said; we need mayors who can make better use of the ample existing powers. Sewell agreed, and feared that citizens would have even more trouble being heard in the system as strong mayors would conclude they didn't need to listen. But they were outnumbered by the advocates of greater mayoral powers, many of whom thought that there had been a glorification of the bygone days of Crombie and Sewell, a time when the city was smaller, simpler, and more manageable.

Crombie and Sewell's objections point out the difficulty of finding the right changes when it comes to powers for cities, and for the right place for cities to occupy in Canada's constitutional firmament. These two are tremendously knowledgeable, and understand both the theory and practice of municipal government. They look at these issues, and come up with very different views on powers from people as well versed as they are. The fact is that people who worry about the relative lack of powers for cities agree with each other on probably 90 percent of the agenda for change. But that last 10 percent can be crippling.

That last 10 percent can become the cudgel with which those who resist change can bludgeon reform. Who resists reform? Those who have something to lose, like provincial finance departments that fear a loss of revenue, provincial bureaucrats who fear loss of authority, federal finance officials who fear the loss of what they have come to think of as "their" money. So, when disagreements between city advocates pop up, they intone the advice that the cities "get their houses in order" before they will even contemplate change. They paint a picture of municipal governments as disorganized, inept, unruly, and occasionally corrupt. "Getting the house in order" is an admonition, tinged with superiority, from levels of government that presume to be models of propriety and probity. This, of course, ignores what we read in the newspapers every day as federal and provincial auditors general report on the boondoggles in Ottawa and the provincial capitals—the gun registry and the sponsorship scandal, or the Ontario Hydro scandal or "Bingo-gate" in British Columbia. All governments could do better, just as all businesses or hospitals or universities or churches could. But the superior tone adopted by federal politicians like federal Finance minister Jim Flaherty or former Ontario Finance minister Greg Sorbara emanates from a shaky source, one that does not bear scrutiny.

The only effective intervention in such a dynamic is from a political superior. The City of Toronto Act happened because Premier Dalton McGuinty made it happen, overriding various objections in his government and its bureaucracy. And reform in British Columbia only happens because two former Vancouver mayors, Mike Harcourt and Gordon Campbell, became premiers of the province and saw what needed to be done.

The Powers of a Province for Big-City Regions

Whether city powers are increased incrementally—one by one as their need is identified and agreement is negotiated—or more broadly by a fundamental change in the relationship, it will still not be enough to satisfy some advocates for change. At least for the large urban regions in the country, there is an argument to be made for a whole new definition of those regions. In effect, the Vancouver, Toronto, and Montreal regions should have the powers of a province. Advocates of this view note that if Prince Edward Island, with its 140,000 residents, can have those powers, the urban regions can. There are almost thirty cities in Canada with larger populations than PEI. Indeed, the Toronto Community Housing Corporation has more residents than PEI.

But the argument is best made not on numbers, because PEI is an anomaly of history, and the country has obviously grown disproportionately due to history, geography, and distribution of natural resources. It is best made on the basis of a difference between a region and the provincial context in which is exists. And the argument would be that Vancouver, Toronto, and Montreal are substantively different than British Columbia, Ontario, and Quebec. Much more so than Edmonton and Calgary are different than Alberta or Halifax is different than Nova Scotia, although the latter example is changing rapidly.

In Toronto, for example, which accepts almost half of Canada's new immigrants each year and whose population is close to half visible minority and half immigrant, that diversity puts different demands on the education and health care systems, both of which are under provincial control. If the province adopts a "one size fits all" approach for the province, it will fit only one or neither. For example, under the Harris government in Ontario, the ministry of education was ordered to scrap all anti-racism programs in the schools. Elected primarily outside the diverse Toronto area, the Harris people thought this programming was an ideological frill, and the minister and deputy minister were told in no uncertain terms to cut it out. It wasn't missed in less racially diverse areas outside of Toronto, where it had been given a passing nod in any case, but less than a decade later there was clear evidence of racial isolation and violence in racial groups, which education experts traced back to the ending of those programs—and to the cutting back at the same time of English as a Second Language programs and other services aimed at making diversity work. When in the summer of 2005 there was an outbreak of gun violence in the Jamaican-Canadian community, experts looked back to those provincial decisions of the mid-'90s. And when a cell of young Muslim Canadians with terrorist plans was uncovered in 2006, so too did attention go to the mid-'90s decisions.

Cutting those programs was not a decision that would have been made in Toronto, either by a Toronto school board or a local government. It would not have been made in any of the surrounding municipalities, like Mississauga with its huge South Asian population or Markham with its large Asian population, or any of the others with their vibrant diverse mix. Not for any ideological reason, at any rate, because they live diversity on the ground, every day, and have a long experience and rich knowledge in making diversity work.

The Cultural Imperatives of Health Care

Similarly, in health care, diversity requires new approaches. Within the medical profession there is a steady increase in awareness of new pathologies and of the need to change treatment protocols.

In recent years, the world has had a sudden awakening to new pathologies, as diseases and germs have arrived from halfway around the world. SARS, West Nile virus, Creutzfeldt-Jakob disease, bird flu, bovine spongiform encephalopathy or mad cow disease, and AIDS have all arrived from afar, catching the Western world and North Americans by surprise, and setting laboratories into a mad scramble to find treatments. Many commentators now predict that Armageddon will arrive as a germ, not a band of terrorists or an airborne nuclear missile.

These germs originate in a small number of places in the world. Toronto-based health activist Jay Godsall says there are a relative handful of sources of these germs, in hot, wet climates. They are transported easily on human bodies or in food, can arrive in Vancouver or Montreal as easily as any passenger arriving from tropical Africa or Asia, and can move from person to person on a sneeze, handshake, or kiss. As the global movement of people and goods becomes ever easier and new points of origin and destination proliferate, so does the chance for germs to migrate. Godsall has been trying to alert the world to this movement, and has been urging the Canadian government to locate a global centre for germ communication in Toronto—which he thinks, because of its position as the most diverse city in the world, is the natural hub. In Godsall's compelling vision, Toronto would be the communication centre that would link the dozen or so primary sources of infectious disease with the thousands of places where they might travel. Using a system of wireless communication, those places that are sources of germs would be able to identify them as they developed, after analyzing what was making people sick locally, and communicate that information to the hub, which would then broadcast it to the network. This would provide early warning, allowing scientists to begin work on antidotes immediately, rather than getting no warning and having to focus all their energy on dealing with a crisis.

Godsall has had trouble convincing governments to undertake his vision, which is quite low tech and low cost, in that it primarily connects existing resources. When the Canadian government finally did wake up to the threat posed by germs, their response was a classic replay of old political solutions. Rather than put the International Centre for Infectious Disease in Toronto (or even Vancouver would have made sense) where there was diversity, eight times the volume of airport arrivals, a critical mass of scientists and doctors experienced with infectious disease, and a number of institutions poised to act, it was put in Winnipeg, which had political advantages that apparently outweighed the practical ones. Even constructing field facilities at the tropical sources of infections would be relatively inexpensive, a matter of constructing a set of campuses that could monitor local health situations and do basic biological analysis.

What Jay Godsall has seen is the new world of medical reality, where the diseases we know run the risk of being pushed aside by diseases we never anticipated, and which we don't know. SARS was a particularly devastating example, hitting Vancouver and Toronto hard. Severe Acute Respiratory Syndrome began in China in November 2002, and the Chinese government failed to report it to anyone until the first cases began to pop up elsewhere four months later. That was when the first cases began to show up in North America, and Toronto got its first case in February 2003, while the first case appeared in Vancouver the next month. Most of the cases that went around the world seem to have originated from the ninth floor of the Hotel Metropole in Kowloon, Hong Kong. Hospitals immediately went into defensive mode, restricting access to visitors and implementing strict hand-washing regimes for everyone coming and going. Canada's tourism industry, like most other places, was just beginning to recover from the 2001 terrorist acts in New York and Washington, but they immediately took a big hit as people cancelled vacations and businesses cancelled meetings and conventions. In March 2003, the Toronto tourism board announced that one third of the city's tourism workers had been laid off. In April 2003, Toronto tourism revenues were down 45 percent, with Vancouver's off 22 percent, Ottawa's 16 percent, Montreal's 14 percent, and Calgary's 13 percent. Three years later, in 2006, there were still restaurants in those cities, mostly those just outside the downtown business district, who say their business has never fully recovered, even though SARS has faded as a health concern. And they are all fully aware that all it would take is just one more germ arriving at Pearson, Trudeau, or Macdonald-Cartier airport for it all to happen again.

And of course, once the germ does arrive, and a patient appears at a doctor's office or hospital with a set of symptoms, doctors face the challenge of figuring out what is wrong. Doctors play an elaborate guessing game, albeit one for which they are uniquely qualified. They match symptoms with possible causes, gradually eliminating options as they observe more and more. But basically they are winnowing based on what they know, and if there is a new disease out there from a new germ, they will have more trouble pinpointing it, and even more trouble deciding on a cure. This is where they need the medical system to be flexible and responsive.

A health care system that understands the new global world will be more likely to offer that flexibility. And it is in the city regions that these new demands will arise, because that is where the people who come from around the world live, and it is where the disease will arrive. If a provincial government can only grant a degree of flexibility that a compromise between all the jurisdictions across their province would allow, it will be less likely to afford the responsiveness that the doctor facing that mysteriously ill patient needs. So more local control over how health care dollars are spent can actually lead to an appropriately responsive system.

Similarly, a diverse population requires different protocols of care. In many cases, there are language barriers, so there is a need for translators. And there may also be a need for some interpretation, beyond just getting the words right. Most urban hospitals have significant resources available for translation and interpretation, often tailored to the demographic profile of the neighbourhoods they serve. Anyone who has had to seek medical help while travelling in a country whose language they don't speak knows how important it is to be able to describe a problem effectively. And a patient's description is an important piece of evidence for a doctor.

Another important component of health care in diverse communities is the attitude of health care professionals—the doctors, nurses, technicians, and all other staff. Hospital and medical office staffs are increasingly being given training to make sure that their attitudes and expressions are not inadvertently racist or prejudicial. While such training is not usually called "anti-racist," because we never like to name it such, that is essentially what it is.

There is also a great focus on culturally appropriate behaviour. In some cultures, there are strong traditions around modesty, gender roles, and other personal matters. In many cases there are reasons why these cannot be observed—for example, if an emergency procedure must be undertaken to save a life or prevent a complication and no female doctor is available, while the patient might have a cultural or religious prohibition against been treated by a man. But the more aware of cultural norms that medical staff are, the easier it becomes to negotiate the best levels of care under the circumstances. Thus, there is an increased focus on fields like medical anthropology, transcultural psychology, and the health beliefs and behaviours of specific groups. Some argue that the tried and true approach of standard medical interrogatory procedures will find a way over cultural bridges, but health care is increasingly looking to bolster those practices with new approaches.

These challenges arise in the diverse city regions. It is important that urban medical practitioners develop these new management skills. But it is less important that rural practitioners do. A single policy would not be appropriate, so the provincial health care system should be able to do what is appropriate, and fund each.

The development of cultural awareness and effectiveness does cost money. Staff for interpretation and translation costs more. It takes time for cultural awareness training, and time is a valuable commodity in health care. Budget allocations must take account of these new challenges, and local control will best assure that the system can provide the most appropriate response to patient needs. Medical practitioners and public health officials in the major cities recognize this new reality of health care and can quickly react to it. But if they need to negotiate compromises between parts of the health care system with dramatically different realities, the delays can result in worse care and can lead to feelings of exclusion on the part of newcomers who encounter unnecessary language and cultural barriers.

Immigrant Settlement Is a Prime City Issue

Immigrant settlement itself is another area in which large city regions are distinct. About 50 percent of Canada's immigrants settle in the Toronto region, with over half the rest going to Vancouver and Montreal. It makes sense, because these places are where the work is, and where people from their culture and who speak their language are. This has long been so, and cities have developed experience and expertise in settling immigrants. Settlement would be more effective if cities had much more power in both policy and program design. But the federal government tends to dominate in policy and program, and spends its money differentially between cities—again, a problem of politics trumping practicality. In some cases the money is sent to the provinces for distribution, but as in most such transfers there is no guarantee that it will be used in the programs—or in the locales—for which it is designated. And at any rate, the money may be earmarked for programs that the city doesn't see as a priority anyway.

From time to time, cities run out of transitional housing for immigrants and refugees, places where they can stay while they search for work and get their housing, schooling, and living arrangements sorted out. Often newcomers find themselves housed on the outskirts of town, and even outside of town. In 2003, some in the Toronto region were being housed in motels in St. Thomas, about 125 miles away, where there were no programs, jobs, or likelihood that they would settle there. Transitional housing for immigrants is a priority need for cities that receive a lot of them, and if those cities had a choice of how to spend money it might well be on the provision of adequate accommodation that would ease and accelerate settlement.

Local governments are often most familiar with the local labour market as well, and they are likely to be able to involve local employers in settlement. The biggest single factor in successful immigrant settlement is the ability to find a good job, one for which the employee has training and experience. The federal and provincial governments might have relationships with large national employers, but the bulk of employment opportunities are in small business, and cities have a great awareness of who is out there, through licensing and other municipal functions. Local governments would be more likely to support, or even initiate, programs to link newcomers to the labour market. Early support for the Toronto Region Immigrant Employment Council, a privately run and locally developed program, came from Toronto mayor David Miller, who had been chair of the city council immigration committee and was sensitive to the critical importance of good labour market linkages. Other governments subsequently came on board and have been critical in TRIEC's success, but the early design and support arose from local awareness and concern.

There is no question that some powers, as well as some responsibilities, rightly reside with federal and provincial governments. The chapter on finance will examine some of the crucial fiscal reasons why everything does not get devolved locally. The principle of "subsidiarity," which says that responsibilities should move either down to the local level or up to the national level, depending on the likelihood of the best outcomes, depends on the ability of linked levels of government to reapportion by agreement. Subsidiarity was an important consideration in the formation of the European Economic Union, but its lessons have not spread abroad easily. For things to change, some levels of government will have to stop doing things while others begin, but that has not been the hard part—both the federal and provincial levels in Canada have been prepared to stop doing things, giving birth to the "downloading" of various obligations during the 1990s. Giving up the revenues that used to pay for those things is the hard part. Money trumps power, it seems, but the power has been hard to budge, too. True change will link money and power, and will require changes in the structure of governance as well. Are Canadian governments up to it? Are Canadian politicians sufficiently visionary and brave?

5

A LASTING, RICH REWARD
How to Pay Our Own Way

"Follow the money" was the crucial piece of advice that "Deep Throat" offered *Washington Post* reporter Bob Woodward as he sought to crack the Watergate scandal. It is good advice.

Corporate denizens know that if you want to find out what a company does, and what it believes, you have to look at where they allocate their financial resources. It is probably true in households, too. By looking at how we spend our money, we can tell whether we believe in the long-term future of our kids, or in our own worldly pleasures. College funds, or swimming pools? The same is certainly true with governments. A simple look at provincial budgets will tell you that their main jobs are to deliver health care services and to run schools. A look at the federal budget will tell you that the main jobs of the national government are to fund benefits for seniors, children, and the unemployed, and to shift money to the provinces for health care and education (these things account for half of the budget).

In fact, financial structure defines most situations, and even the most complex ones can be rendered more comprehensible by a close observation of the financial arrangements.

In Canada, our tax system forms the spine of our government arrangements. The bulk of government revenues comes from taxation, collected through the income tax, sales tax, and a set of excise taxes. Excise taxes are levied on a range of products like alcohol, tobacco products, and gasoline. Income tax is by far the biggest revenue producer, generating almost 65 percent of the federal government's revenues (personal income tax makes up about 47 percent, while corporate income tax contributes about 15 percent), with sales tax next at 15 percent. Excise taxes, tariffs on traded goods, revenues from Crown corporations, and other fees account for the remaining 20 percent of revenues. Provincial budgets show a similar dominant impact of income taxes, with sales tax being the next largest, but still important, component of total revenues.

There is lively debate about whether our taxation system is based on proper values, and there are proponents of "tax shifting." Their argument is that we are taxing "good" things like income and trade, two positive aspects of a capitalist economy, and thereby providing a disincentive. What we should do is tax bad things, like pollution, excessive energy consumption, garbage, and the externalizing of the costs of development (such as the cost of connecting housing subdivisions to roads, sewers, and power lines). Tax shifters want to give positive incentives to good things, and negative incentives to bad things. An appealing idea, it is a bridge too far for contemporary Canadian governments to consider.

While governments find taxation a productive and effective source of revenue, collecting it is a significant and expensive administrative task. Thus, by agreement with the provinces, the federal government collects the money, then distributes some of it to the provinces. There are exceptions to this arrangement, primarily Quebec, which has its own collection system. Collecting tax efficiently is a critical function for governments, and Canadian governments are relatively good at it, not that this is likely to win them many accolades from citizens.

When tax experts like Enid Slack at the University of Toronto's Institute on Municipal Finance and Governance evaluate a proposed tax, they look for a number of criteria:

- The tax should not drive people away to another jurisdiction, so the population to be taxed needs to be relatively unlikely to move to avoid the tax.
- The tax should yield sufficient revenue to pay for the needs it is being raised for, and the yield should increase as the need increases.
- The yield should also be stable and predictable, not based on something either highly cyclical or temporary.
- The tax should apply to those receiving the benefit of the service it will pay for, and not to those who won't benefit, such as non-residents of a district.
- It should be visible and accountable, clear that it is being paid and with clear political and bureaucratic responsibility for being spent on the needs for which it is being raised.
- The tax should be fair, proportionate both to the services it is paying for and to the taxpayer's ability to pay it.
- It should be relatively easy to administer.[*]

Most of the taxes Canadians pay meet most of these criteria. If all three levels of government had access to a wide range of taxes, citizens might not be happy, but they would be served by a fair and effective tax regime.

---

[*] *Reprinted from Enid Slack, "Revenue Sharing Options for Canada's Hub Cities," (Enid Slack Consulting Inc., 2004).*

But the problem for Canadian cities is that they don't have access to a broad range of taxes, but are instead overly reliant on one tax, the property tax. Canadian cities rely on property tax for about 50 percent of their revenues, compared to 15 percent for US cities and 5 percent for European cities. We are not the only country in the world whose cities are so reliant on property tax. Generally, cities in the British Commonwealth countries have a heavy reliance on property tax, while northern European countries have a heavy reliance on income tax, and southern European countries rely on a broader mix of property, income, sales, and other taxes. Cities in the United States vary widely; some are highly dependent on property tax, while others have a broad array of revenue tools, including income and sales taxes, and a good mix of debt instruments.

Property tax meets many of the criteria people like Enid Slack look for, but it misses in a few important ways. It does not grow with the economy, because property values grow relatively slowly, whereas in a booming economy incomes grow quickly—in two ways, in fact, as individual incomes rise, while the total amount of income earned grows as the workforce increases in size—and sales tax revenue grows quickly as more people buy more goods and services. Property taxes also do not necessarily reflect a person's ability to pay them. Take the case of a school teacher who buys a house in a neighbourhood, perhaps near the school where they are teaching, and owns that house for thirty years. If the neighbourhood gentrifies, or just generally increases in value as the town or city grows up around it, and if the tax is levied on the market value of the property, the property tax may consume a larger and larger proportion of that teacher's budget each year until they are forced to sell the house and downscale. That market value assessment, some argue, may also discourage investment in improving a property—say, by adding a new bedroom, porch, or swimming pool—for fear of jacking up the tax bill.

Fixing the revenue deficiency for city governments is a difficult task. In the first place, it needs the approval and participation of another level of government, probably both provincial and federal. Second, it would have to gain the approval of the citizens of the city, because it is certain that any new tax authority in a city would be countered by an anti-tax crusader who would know that such a stance has for years been the ticket to power. A mayor or council that proposed a new tax revenue source—say, a city income tax or a city sales tax—would find a vibrant and well-supported opposition at the next election. Exactly such a situation played out in Toronto in the summer of 2007, when anti-tax factions delayed the addition of two new taxes despite their obvious necessity in meeting a half-billion-dollar budget deficit.

Ideally, a new revenue source would arise out of cooperation between different levels of government. For example, the federal government might say that it does not need to collect all of the revenue from income tax it now collects, given a decade of robust surpluses, and will lower federal income tax by, say, one percent for any citizen living in a city that agrees to implement an income tax of the same amount. Or a similar arrangement could be made with a provincial government around income or sales tax, or perhaps a provincial liquor tax. If this happened, taxpayers would not be paying any more tax than they are now, but governments with less need would cede tax "room" to those with more need.

This is different than what happened when the federal government of Stephen Harper reduced the Goods and Services Tax by one percentage point in 2006 and another point in 2007. It did this unilaterally with the intention of reaping public acclaim and political capital for being "tax cutters." Had Harper's government recognized the financial plight of the big cities, or chosen to cooperate with the cities for other reasons, it might have coordinated that tax cut with an opportunity for cities to take over the taxing capacity.

But politicians at different levels in Canada don't look for opportunities to cooperate. They look for small political wins instead, and country-building takes a kick in the slats when they do. Typically, when cities say they need more revenue, federal finance ministers and prime ministers, and many provincial finance ministers, have told them to "get their financial houses in order"—surprising advice, given the regular reports from their own auditors general about the fiscal disorder in the federal and provincial houses. In fact, most finance officials at the federal and provincial levels view the tax revenues they get as "their" money, and wonder why anyone should expect that they would part with any of it, no matter what other needs might be out there. The more strident the requests for federal or provincial funding get, the more righteous the refusals become.

In effect, those levels of government are addicted to the plentiful revenues that are produced in the parts of the country that create the most wealth, primarily the cities, and the rising cries to get more of it back are disconcerting to them. Federal politicians spread this money around the country for projects that are often worthy and could not be funded without the contributions of the wealthier parts of Canada. It is the money that makes politics work, and that supports governments and government workers. And it has come to be seen as a right of those who receive it and spend it. Any threatened interruption in that supply of money is met with the reactions of those with an addiction whose supply is threatened: denial, anger, and blaming of the victim. Cities are told that there is no problem, and certainly not one that the federal or provincial government in question owns a part of. They are scorned for portraying another level of government unfairly.

And they are told that the real problem lies in their own inability to manage, to get their house in order, and to stop squandering all the structural and instrumental advantages that have been bestowed upon them.

There is no doubt, of course, that municipal governments can do more to use the tools that are available to them, and that they could do a better job managing their affairs. In this way they are just like provincial and federal governments, as auditors general at both levels annually point out. But to rely on suboptimal performance by city governments as a reason to avoid change, or a reason to wait, is foolish. And to take any delight at all in the supposed inadequacies of city governments is a crime against country-building, a deliberate hobbling of national potential, and a churlish exercise in spite.

The large-city regions need access to a much broader array of revenue tools. They need to be able to levy taxes that are appropriate to their needs. Some city politicians prefer to receive grants, rather than taxing authority from other governments. In 2006, Toronto mayor David Miller began a campaign for one percentage point of the federal GST collected in Toronto, and other mayors joined the call. But he did not want permission to collect a sales tax, he just wanted the federal government to agree to transfer an amount of money to the city. He set the amount based on the fact that the federal government had already lowered the GST by one percentage point and intended to reduce it by an additional point (which it did in the budget brought down in autumn 2007). Cynics would say that the mayors had chosen the easy way out, but would also point out that their proposal would not be that attractive to the federal government of Stephen Harper, which relished its tax-cutting reputation. By getting the federal government to hand over the equivalent of a tax cut, the cities would appear not to be levying a tax, but at the same time the federal government would not be reducing citizens' overall tax burden. The result would be a clear win for the cities, but not the federal Conservatives.

Tax analysts generally would suggest that the proper way to shift the revenue stream would be for the federal government to lower the GST by the one or two points it wanted, and for the cities to have permission to levy a sales tax if they so chose. Thus, the cities would have to make a case for the new tax, perhaps by articulating what the money would be applied to (improved services, waterfront development, assisted housing for homeless people) and taking the political heat for it.

The worst thing about poaching another government's tax base is that there is always the risk that that government could cut you off. So, in the case of the 1 percent campaign, the federal government might decide to do it for a few years, and then abruptly stop. And they might stop during an economic downturn, when city needs might be at their highest. The city has no control of its destiny.

But if the city has the authority to levy its own taxes, and a broad mix of taxes, it is much more in control of its destiny, and much more able to predict its future revenues, and therefore to plan.

In addition to the property tax on which they presently rely so heavily, Canadian cities should be able to levy income tax, payroll tax, a general retail sales tax, and special excise taxes on liquor sales, hotel rooms, parking spaces, tobacco products, and whatever other things they might want to influence or control the use of. They should be able to charge tolls to use their roads and add licensing surcharges for vehicle registrations. And they should be able to issue a range of debt instruments, such as municipal bonds and other financing tools.

With regard to taxes, there is no sign that Canadian cities are champing at the bit to use these taxes. Most mayors and councils would probably say they don't want them. Just send us the money, please, they would say, preferably with no strings attached. Even were there to be a group of mayors who would pick up such tax tools, it is unlikely they would be applied aggressively, at least at the outset. If the tools were available to cities, though, it is more likely that a province and city would be able to agree to a shift in revenue streams, particularly as part of the regular discussions they have about which level of government is best suited to delivering which set of services. Such discussions are a normal feature of provincial-municipal conversations at both the bureaucratic and political levels, and evolving circumstances often change the service-delivery equation. Having a similar set of revenue tools at both levels of government would make the reassignment of tasks much easier to execute. And such a "trading" capacity between levels of government would make it much easier to shift responsibilities in a tax-neutral way, so that anti-tax umbrage might be contained.

Excise taxes are a good way to both control behaviour and express values. Ontarians and British Columbians pay high taxes on imported wine because those provinces have robust wine industries that the provinces protect. Canadians generally pay high taxes on alcohol as a hangover from the days when booze was a demon that should be discouraged, but not banned. Taxes on tobacco have risen sharply as evidence of the venality of that industry and its products became apparent. The ability to tax would enable cities to express their values around particular issues, values that might differ from those of other jurisdictions. For example, environmentally conscious Vancouverites might choose to implement high taxes on parking spaces downtown to discourage people from driving into the core of the city, or they might have a licensing surcharge on gas-guzzling and space-hogging sport utility vehicles to encourage the use of smaller and more environmentally friendly vehicles. Victoria already has small street parking spaces for Smart cars, with rates at about a third of normal parking fees. Having access to a broad range of excise taxes, without having to ask permission from another level of government or average out views over a region that might be, for example, more sympathetic to SUVs, makes for more robustly democratic government.

Debt Can Be Useful for Cities

Debt instruments are a particularly interesting opportunity for cities. In fact, a broad range of financing tools is available to those who live in stable financial environments. And it is important to note in this context that cities are incredibly stable places.

There is a famous story told in many places, but nowhere nearly as well as by former Toronto mayor David Crombie, of the prominent Torontonian who was travelling to Italy and wanted to have an audience with the Pope. A lifelong devout Roman Catholic, this was to be the highlight for a man who was known throughout Canada for his business and community achievements. He made application to the Vatican, citing his Canadian roots and connections and including letters of commendation from both the Prime Minister of Canada and the Governor General, both of whom he knew and both of whom were effusive in their recommendations. In due course, and somewhat nervously close to his travel date, he received a letter back from the Vatican secretary asking if he might forward a letter from the mayor of the city he lived in, which was Toronto. Thinking he had covered off the pooh-bah quotient with the PM and the GG, he asked his assistant to double check to make sure this was absolutely required, and they were assured it was. So he got the mayor to send along a recommendation, and he was duly granted an audience with the Pope. While he was at the Vatican, waiting in an anteroom, he was introduced to the Vatican secretary who had made the request for the mayoral letter, and he expressed his interest in the fact that the PM and GG's letters had not been deemed adequate. And the Vatican secretary replied, "Yes, that is a common reaction we get. But we have been around for some centuries, and we know that nations come and go, but cities last forever."

The Roman Catholic Church, as it turns out, is on to something. People who map cities will tell you that, despite all the cranes we might see in our cities during boom times, cities change very slowly and are highly stable places. We read a newspaper story that a company has come to town, or moved to the suburbs, or that a new office tower is going up, but such changes are marginal, effecting well less than 1 percent of the built and traded infrastructure. In New York City, the island of Manhattan has approximately 500 million square feet of office space, but at its peak has built around five million square feet of new space a year, and most years much less. The edges of cities are where growth occurs, but it is typically of such low density—single-family homes on generous lots—that it is a small increment to the existing inventory, although it makes the map grow at the periphery.

In fact, if you take that physical stability, and add to it the tremendous inflow of new residents to our large-city regions, you have the makings of a tantalizing set of commercial opportunities. The Toronto region, for example, has a highly stable physical core, and will add five million people over the next three decades. A business person looking at that would salivate at the potential for productive enterprise, of the sort that best meets the needs of buyer and seller. They would happily go to a banker and arrange financing for all sorts of things that would meet the needs of the new population, all secured by the stability of what is already there. This is, as we know, already being done by the home builders, who are assembling land for the new residents. But as for the waste managers, the fresh water suppliers, the transit providers, the home care and aged care and child care providers—all could take advantage of such an opportunity, but would need financing.

To be able to raise that financing, cities need predictability, particularly around revenue streams. The home builders know that they can assume debt now to assemble land and build houses because there will be buyers down the road, and nobody is going to step between them and the buyer to divert the revenue stream that will retire their debts. Cities don't know that. They might, for example, invest in a new waste-management system, perhaps modelled on the successful Swedish plants that collect and incinerate neighbourhood waste, returning useable energy to the neighbourhood with negligible pollution (much less than what our Canadian landfills produce). But to borrow the money to build the plant, a city government would have to be assured that at some future time another level of government would not take over the revenue stream (the fees householders would pay to the city for waste management), or divert the energy produced by cogeneration away from the particular neighbourhood (on the notion that it was a "provincial good" and should be available to all parts of the province), or outlaw incineration in response to a particularly vigorous political lobby. In other words, there would have to be stability and control of destiny. Otherwise, you would never undertake the risk of the venture, and you would just stick to old technology and old appeals for money, and you would leave a valuable array of financing tools strewn about, unused.

P3s and TIFs: Key Financial Tools

Two financial tools that cities could use more effectively include public-private partnerships, known popularly as P3s, and tax increment financing, or TIFs. Both require stability and predictability to work properly, and both are best used when applied to infrastructure improvements.

P3s in effect create a partnership of private money and expertise with public projects. They cover a wide range of projects from such major infrastructure as roads, bridges, and energy projects to senior-care facilities, schools, and commissaries. The Golden Ears Bridge in greater Vancouver is being built by a partnership of the Greater Vancouver Transportation Authority and Bilfinger Berger (Canada) Inc. It is named after the peaks on Mount Blanshard, which have been known for years as the Golden Ears. When it opens in 2009, it will span one kilometre over the Fraser River, linking Surrey and Langley on the south shore with Maple Ridge and Pitt Meadows on the north. The steel-decked, cable-stayed bridge will cost over $800 million to build. It will be a toll bridge, with tolls collected electronically. Drivers can obtain a transponder to record their presence automatically, or their licence plates can be photographed and vehicle owners billed, like the system in place on the Ontario toll road, Highway 407. (More modern developments in tolling will see electronic chips embedded in licence plates, which can be read either by stationary readers along bridges and highways or by satellites, allowing tolling to be implemented anywhere at any time.) The revenues from tolls will pay for the cost of financing, building, maintaining, and operating the bridge.

Similarly, the expansion of the Sea-to-Sky Highway project for the 2010 Olympic Games in Vancouver and Whistler is a public-private partnership between the BC Ministry of Transportation and Macquarie North America. Macquarie is an Australian merchant bank with financing and technical expertise in a wide range of infrastructure activities. Similarly, the toll highway between Moncton and Fredericton, New Brunswick, which opened in 2001, was a partnership between the provincial department of transportation and the road builder, the Miller Group.

Such partnerships don't only work on big infrastructure projects. The city of Sidney, British Columbia, built the new SHOAL (Sidney Healthy Options for Active Living) Centre, a seniors' recreation centre, in partnership with the SCH Group. And the Ontario ministry for community and social services worked with the management consulting arm of Accenture to redesign and streamline its business processes, resulting in savings and increased efficiency.

Anything that will produce a future stream of revenue, or will reduce costs in a way that does not reduce revenues, can lend itself to public-private partnerships. They can involve a mix of financing, some from public and some from private sources, or a mix of expertise. In many cases, government provides access to a market—say, people who drive across bridges, or who use hospitals or seniors' residences. They can provide expertise as well, around road building and design, health care delivery, or education processes. They also provide a legislative framework that can secure and stabilize an enterprise. The private partner can provide capital, expertise, management capability, and an element of risk taking that governments find uncomfortable.

Not everyone is a fan of P3s. Jane Jacobs famously called them "monstrous hybrids" and warned that the "guardian" or custodian role of governments did not mix easily with the commercial role of business, and that for the two of them to find common cause was wrongheaded. Each should labour in its own mode, true to its instincts and capacities. Blending or diluting their true nature would likely end unhappily. Others argue against them on a financial basis. They say that when you take a basically public project and bring in a private partner, one that requires that a profit be taken, you increase the cost. They reject arguments that the private sector is naturally more cost effective, able to do things better and cheaper. They point to a very large number of public projects that have been done well. They say that P3s are only in fashion because politicians have been cowed into avoiding projects due to their fear of having to raise the funds to complete them, something that would require raising taxes or increasing the public debt. The public has become so set against the idea of government being engaged in great finance that the politicians have wilted.

Tax increment financing (TIF) is another interesting financing tool. The classic TIF spotlights a particular part of a city that could benefit from an infrastructure improvement—perhaps the extension of a transit line into or through it, improvement of street lighting to make a neighbourhood safer and more attractive, or the remediation of the soil in an old industrial area to make it safe for residences and business. Each of these initiatives would be expected to boost the property values of the area, to increase the amount of commercial activity, and to add jobs. Thus there would be increased future revenue from property, sales, and income taxes. Backed by those anticipated revenues, the government could issue municipal bonds. Of course, the amount of the bond issue would be based on the amount of the potential tax revenue, and if a city were limited to the revenue from property tax, it would issue fewer bonds than if it had access to income and sales tax.

One of the problems often cited with TIFs is that they can lead to dislocation of current residents, as the neighbourhood responds to the improvements by gentrification. The older residents move out as property values, and property taxes, rise, replaced by higher-income residents who can afford the increased taxes. This is less a fault of TIFs than of the improvements themselves. TIFs can also bias a city's renewal agenda, inclining it to hold back on projects in areas where it doesn't have bond exposure, even if that area's needs for some reason leap to the fore. But their great advantage is that a city doesn't have to rely on another level of government for money, and it can access the private financial market.

A riff on a TIF, if you will, is to forget the bonds and just levy a special charge on the residents of the area in question, letting them finance up front the improvements that will ultimately benefit them. This might be applied to their property tax, or take the form of a higher sales tax in that area, or an income tax surcharge. These direct charges, while honest and straightforward, are not popular, and can have the effect of driving some people out of the neighbourhood. But there is considerable virtue in making costs as transparent as possible and attributing them as directly as possible to the beneficiaries. As noted elsewhere, allowing the externalization or generalizing of costs can lead to undesirable outcomes, like sprawl and its attendant evils of air pollution and social isolation.

Boundaries and Distortions

When the question of additional revenue sources for cities comes up, there are two questions people ask more than others: Which taxes? And what are the boundaries?

The boundary issue is tricky. Andrew Sancton, a professor at the University of Western Ontario and Canada's leading expert on municipal amalgamations, thinks boundaries are the stick in the spokes of city autonomy, an issue so difficult to resolve in the real world that it not only will stop any change, but will provide justification for leaving municipalities in thrall to provincial governments. Sancton has focused on this issue in recent years, and is publishing an interesting book on it.

If Calgary were to decide to levy a sales tax, in a province that doesn't have one, what would prevent Calgarians from crossing city limits to shop? Operators of gas stations are always amazed at how far someone will drive to save a cent or two per litre to fuel up their car. They'll burn much more than the dollar they save. One solution is to have a region subscribe to the same tax regime. If it is a large enough region, the densities on the borders will be low and the utility of crossing for savings less. And if the boundaries are likely to change, as a municipality on the margin decides to take advantage of the higher tax regime and its revenues, the risk of creating a commercial infrastructure based on the presumed tax-avoiding market will become unattractive to developers.

All taxes have some negative consequences or "distortions," as is well revealed by the work of Enid Slack and Harry Kitchen. They note that the property tax is actually a disincentive to home ownership. But the income tax is an incentive, because the increase in value of the home is not subject to income tax rates. What they recommend is a mix of taxes, each providing its own incentives and disincentives, all of them balancing the others. And if you add in things like road tolls, you can further mitigate some of the downsides of boundary issues as you make it more expensive for people to shop farther away.

They note that taxes can be based on the "benefit" approach, or on the "ability-to-pay" approach. The benefit approach says that those who are likely to benefit should pay the tax. The ability-to-pay approach taxes higher incomes more than lower ones. Some expenditures—say, for welfare programs—don't really lend themselves to the benefit approach and must be based on ability to pay. In such cases, having those taxes levied to any great extent locally may cause wealthier people to seek a less taxing place to live. They'll vote with their feet. But if such a tax is part of a mix of taxes, its effect may be less dramatic than if it were one of few taxes. Ideally, ability-to-pay taxes aimed at things like welfare programs should be levied at the national level, so that those wishing to avoid paying those taxes would have to leave the country, rather than just cross the city line. Leaving the country is a much bigger step. It involves leaving jobs, friends, and vital social and business networks.

A mix of taxes levied at the city level would include property tax, which Canadian cities are already well used to, although there is heated debate on whether it should be based on market value or some notional value that increases incrementally but insulates people of modest income from dramatic spikes in the value of their property, which would raise their taxes abruptly and often force them to move. A city could levy an income tax, a modest surcharge on the provincial or federal tax bill. To use Toronto as an example (other cities might roughly estimate their own figures based on relative population), if the city levied an income tax surcharge equivalent to about 1 percent of taxable income, according to Kitchen and Slack, it would raise close to $500 million, a good contribution to an annual budget of about $7 billion. Levying an additional 1 percent general sales tax would net Toronto about $375 million a year. Specific excise taxes, on liquor, tobacco, or hotel rooms, would be much less lucrative. A one-cent levy on vehicle fuel would yield perhaps $35 million, and most other taxes less. But the mix would spread the burden.

The other vital principle is that the city in question must have the ability to choose which taxes it will levy and at what rates. Having those imposed by a provincial or federal government does not lead to control of destiny, nor does it lead to an ability to use any of the more innovative financing instruments, like P3s or TIFs. The predictability and stability would be absent. And worse, the timidity of city officials, unwilling to risk an uncertain financial future, would remain.

Canadian cities are making do with much less revenue than they need to reach their potential. The large, thriving urban regions have a particular need to be able to invest in those things that will enhance their international competitiveness. Waiting for federal and provincial governments has not worked out very well for them over the past quarter century. They need much broader control of their destinies, and in no area is it more vital than in their ability to raise revenues. They need access to a much broader array of tax and financing instruments, and they need to have the authority to decide what taxes they'll levy, and how much. Without it, they will continue to slip behind, depending on the kindness of strangers to bail them out from year to year.

6

DOMINION
The Right Form of Government to Do the Job

If, some bright, sunlit day, when a warm breeze blew gently at the country's back, the lambs grazed in the full grass fields, and the corner fruit stand stood flush with the bounty of the summer harvest . . . if, on that perfect day, Canadian cities were to get the powers and financial tools they needed, could they do the job?

If they were to be granted a full slate of powers that would permit them to control their destinies, and they were to be allowed to exercise a full range of revenue tools in order to pay for destiny's call, would they be able to exercise them? Would they be able to grasp that moment and begin to realize the full potential of the cities as vital instruments of international competitiveness?

The answer is uncertain, at best. Cities, mayors, and councils have their moments of brilliance. In Toronto, David Crombie, prodded and supported by his council, brought in a bylaw for new buildings that set a height limit of forty-five feet. The bylaw stopped a rampant development industry in its tracks and set the stage for the preservation of neighbourhoods that are still a defining feature of the city. A few decades later, Mayor Barbara Hall designated the Kings, an area to the west of the financial district, for accelerated planning approvals that served to rapidly renew and invigorate a key area of the city. In Vancouver, Mayor Philip Owen courageously and with great vision embraced the modern Four Pillars Drug Strategy for the treatment of drug addiction, support that eventually cost him the nomination of his backward-looking municipal party and the mayoralty. In Montreal, new mayor Gerald Tremblay convened an all-sector summit to create an atmosphere of collaborative action for the city. So, cities can get things right.

And they can run things well. The Toronto Community Housing Corporation, wholly owned by the City of Toronto, is one of the largest housing operations in the world, with 165,000 tenants. More people live in TCHC housing than in all but twenty Canadian cities. It is well run by Derek Ballantyne, one of the most talented business managers in Canada. Montreal's excellent Botanical Garden (Jardin Botanique de Montréal) is another well-run civic asset, and it even provided Montreal with a mayor when its director, Pierre Bourque, was elected in 1994. And it takes an exception like Walkerton, Ontario, which mismanaged its water supply so tragically, to remind us that Canadian cities are particularly good at providing plentiful and clean drinking water to households.

So it is easy to cite examples of mayors, councils, and public servants getting things right. In fact, around the world people look to Canadian cities as sources of know-how. For years, the Canadian Urban Institute (CUI) has had a vibrant program that sought lessons in best practice from other places and also arranged for municipal officials from other countries to visit Canadian cities to learn how they managed water and sewage, roads and traffic, bookkeeping and accounting, property tax collection, social services and public health, and the myriad other services cities provide. And Canadian municipal managers travelled abroad under CUI auspices to the Baltic states, eastern Europe, and Asia to share knowledge. By most accounts, Canadian cities are well managed.

But in the area of governance, the story is not as good. And the extent to which Canadian cities have slipped in recent decades and let their competitive guard down can be traced to issues of governance. The structure of local government, in particular the relationship of mayor to council, is one key issue. Another is whether councillors are elected on a ward basis, or on a city-wide basis, a difference that can have a major effect on the quality of vision put into play. The presence or absence of political parties at the municipal level can also play an important part in the ability to move forward.

This conversation is, for the most part, about our largest cities, where mayors and councillors work full time. In most of Canada's 4,500 municipalities, mayors and councillors work part time, holding down other jobs or living on retirement incomes, while fulfilling duties of office during the evenings or lunch times. The local tax base, and perhaps the local political culture, doesn't support the higher salaries that go with full-time engagement, and some would argue that the issues, while not necessarily less complex or important, don't pop up as frequently.

The Weak Mayor System

Canadian cities are generally governed by what is known as a "weak-mayor" system. The mayor may be the only member of city council elected on a city-wide basis, but she has slightly more powers than any other member of council. (In most cities, every voter gets to cast a vote for a mayor, while councillors are elected only by the voters of a particular ward or district.) Once the election is over, and council sits, the mayor may act as chair of council, and may have a larger office and a few more assistants, and certainly has more ribbons to cut and dinners to attend. But on substantive issues, the mayor is just another member of council, with only one vote. Thus, a good part of the time of a "weak mayor" is spent cobbling together support for the initiatives in which she is interested. Sometimes, if the stars align, she can put together a coalition that will span a range of issues and last over a period of several votes. But often a new deal has to be put together on every issue, which can be enervating and time consuming. In a politically volatile environment, where differing views or ambitions prevail, such constant deal-making can be terribly restrictive, limiting what a municipal government can achieve. All too often in city council chambers across the country, marathon sessions drag late into the night, bogged down in rambling commentary, wild digressions, and ad hominem thrusts. As the demands on cities grow—legitimate demands for the infrastructure and services that will allow citizens to thrive and compete—city councils often diminish their capacity by becoming victims of their structure.

There are a number of advantages of a weak-mayor system. It does not allow too much power to fall into the hands of one person, and for those who subscribe to Lord Acton's dictum that absolute power corrupts absolutely, this is a good thing. For the mayor to have to seek and find allies for her ambitions is salutary. Many people agree with former Toronto mayor David Crombie, who has said that a weak-mayor system is less of a problem than weak mayors. This implies that a mayor with sufficient gusto can be highly effective, without the downside that moving to a strong-mayor system brings. The weak-mayor system also leads to stronger councillors, who are able to become strong leaders and advocates for the interests of their wards. In most such systems, councillors tend to respect the primacy of other councillors as representatives of their wards, and will likely support the ward initiatives they bring forward. And because there is no singular, over-whelming seat of power, citizens feel they can approach council with some possibility of influencing outcomes, which is why most cities have a regular opportunity for the public to make deputations directly to council and its committees. Those who like the weak-mayor system view these attributes to be essential virtues of democracy. In fact, they talk about the municipal level of government in a weak-mayor frame-work as being a great expression of democracy, where citizens have the most direct access to government and its work.

Others think such views are a confection of pieties. They note that the opposite of a weak mayor is not necessarily an absolute dictator, and that there are many ways to circumscribe power through effec-tive council oversight, through bylaws that require matters of material interest to be subject to supermajority approval, through fiscal trans-parency, through administrative procedures, and ultimately through the courts. They note that empowered councillors can become tyrants in their own right, exercising great influence over development in their wards and controlling what goes forward from the ward for approval by council. And they observe that the public access to council works better in theory than practice, that most public deputations penetrate council deliberations like water off a duck's back, and that influenc-ing council is still a matter of making the right back-room deal with the right set of councillors.

The Strong-Mayor System

Cities such as New York, London, and Chicago have a "strong-mayor" system, where the mayor has substantially more powers than council-lors, and has the necessary political and administrative support to be able to articulate and achieve an agenda. The budget permits the hir-ing of high-level, competent staff for the mayor's office, in much the same way that a provincial, federal, or state cabinet minister or head of state might. The mayor might have control over appointments to key council committees and senior positions in the public service, and would be responsible for preparing an annual plan and budget for the city, subject to the approval of the council. The mayor would have a powerful ability to articulate a vision for the city, and she and her team would be able to propose a plan to realize that vision. It would not be a team vision and plan prepared by council through a process of consensus seeking, but one driven from the office of the mayor.

There are advantages to this arrangement, particularly if the mayor in question has sufficient powers and the city has access to sufficient revenue sources. As the highly successful businessman Michael Bloomberg discovered when he became mayor of New York, the external perception of the mayor's office as a place where things can actually be done attracts people of ambition and competence. Bloomberg could appoint a number of deputy mayors, which in New York are non-elected people who head up various parts of the city administration. He had met former investment banker Dan Doctoroff when the latter recruited him to support the New York bid to host the 2012 Olympic Games, which Doctoroff had initiated in the mid-1990s. Bloomberg was impressed with Doctoroff's drive and ability, and invited him to become deputy mayor for economic development. After some hesitation, Doctoroff accepted, at a salary of $1 per year, and set about overseeing sixty-two projects in Manhattan, including the development of the devastated World Trade Center site and the reimagining of Governor's Island, the former military enclave off the tip of Manhattan. Doctoroff, and people like him in other cities, take on such "pro bono" work for love of the city, love of the challenge, and to be part of the action. Reporting directly to the mayor, and not dependent on his paycheque, Doctoroff has become a powerful force in land use, zoning, and development decisions in the city. Too powerful for some, who yearn for more accountability and for city council to be able to rein him in.

This is the big threat of the strong-mayor system. A good or at least benign dictator can be easy to take. But a bad or malevolent one can be a nightmare. In the context of New York, people point to Jane Jacobs and her distaste for the reign of Robert Moses, the legendary New York state and city builder. Moses never held elective office, having been trounced in his one run for the governorship of New York state. But he held a succession of appointed offices, first by New York governor Al Smith and later by a succession of New York City mayors. His usual perch was as head of the parks commission, but he took on a vast array of other appointments to build bridges and utilities and expressways, and managed to spread his domain through unmatched energy and ability. He made even Doctoroff look like a piker by comparison: in 1933, in his first two months as city parks director under Mayor Fiorello La Guardia, he completed 1,700 projects, according to architectural critic Paul Goldberger. It wasn't always pretty. He evicted great numbers of poor people in order to raze slums and rebuild them. His ambitious building of neighbourhood parks never seemed to penetrate black or Hispanic neighbourhoods. Critics gave him a verbal thrashing, laced with biblical and Shakespearian references. Jacobs viewed him as a destroyer of neighbourhoods, an addict of the megaproject that often ignored and overrode local context and desire. But he reigned supreme, good and bad, for decades, unchallenged by a succession of weak mayors who followed La Guardia, and who managed to work well with him, until he ran into Governor Nelson Rockefeller, who held that office for fifteen years from 1958 until 1973. Rockefeller gradually took away Moses' positions, leaving him powerless. Ironically, Moses is the salutary lesson both for those opposed to and in favour of stronger executive authority in mayor's offices. If you like what he accomplished, which was a lot, you are in favour; if not, Moses is the spectre.

The "Stronger" Mayor

Toronto is trying something in the middle, the "stronger-mayor system." In revisions to the City of Toronto Act proclaimed on the first day of 2007, the province strengthened the role of the mayor, without going to the full extent of creating a US- or London-style strong-mayor system. The process had been started several years before, with staff-level discussions between the province and city. When the framework of the revised Act was settled, the city appointed an advisory panel of outsiders (community college president Ann Buller, constitutional lawyer and law professor Sujit Choudhry, and businessman Martin Connell) to advise on changes to city governance. Council subsequently adopted the bulk of the recommendations, which principally served to create more executive authority in the mayor's office and clearer lines of accountability. The changes took place after municipal elections in late 2006, in time for the new council's first meeting in 2007.

The main changes are that the mayor gets to select the members of the executive committee, and has control over appointing committee chairs and senior staff, including the city manager, the top civil servant. The mayor can also appoint one or more deputy mayors, but they must be sitting members of council. The mayor is responsible for the preparation of the annual budget for the city—formerly a task of the whole council, which engaged in a long and enervating process of horse trading and favour swapping. There are, of course, some legitimate benefits to trading and swapping. It identifies interests with those promoting them, moderation often emerges, and many voices are heard. At the same time, vision tends to be blunted, half-measures get embraced, and high-quality initiatives can give way to resources being spread too thinly in the name of fairness. In the first budget prepared under the stronger-mayor regime, much concern was expressed about things being done behind closed doors, at least in the budget-preparation phase. As it turned out, a lot of people preferred to see their sausage made in public, even if it made the result a little less palatable.

The other big change in process was the election of councillors and the mayor for terms of four years rather than three.

The intent of the changes to the Act, as well as others by city council to its own procedures, was to create more effective city government. There were a number of reasons to do so. One was the simple fact that the city had become larger and more complicated. The forced amalgamation of 1997 upset both politics and administration, and the gradual settling on both those dimensions showed that some changes in design would help. Another reason was the province's concern that government needed to be conducted more responsibly at the municipal level, or there would be no hope that the city could be sustainable without regular appeals to the province for funds. There was a strong feeling in some parts of the Ontario government that successive administrations at Toronto City Hall had failed to exercise enough fiscal discipline in cutting costs and rationalizing programs. One of the principal sticking points was the high degree of unionization of city services, which some ideologues at the province believed had ratcheted up costs and ground down service. This was, in large part, the same sentiment that had led to amalgamation in the first place: that a newer, bigger city government was needed to face down the unions and take on more responsibilities. The amalgamation had been done quite stupidly, mostly because of some last-minute meddling on the part of the premier that resulted in the costs of social services being downloaded onto the city. The renovations of 2006–07 were a more benign government's attempts to create a stable platform from which the city could take more control over its own turf.

It will be some years before it is evident whether a "stronger-mayor" system is better or worse than either weak or strong systems. And matters will be complicated by the question of whether the system or the mayor is responsible for the way things play out. As former mayor Crombie said, what we need is a strong mayor. But we don't always get our wish, and sometimes we have to rely on a system. A mediocre mayor can be surrounded by good committee chairs and an active and lively council. In a system with the proper oversights, checks, and balances, the worst of a bad mayor can be avoided. And the best of a good mayor can be enhanced. Crombie, a good mayor, is a good example. He was surrounded, prodded, and supported by an active and bright cadre of councillors, and the combination served the city well, in what many still consider its golden age. It will take several terms of stronger mayors in Toronto, perhaps a decade's worth, for the city to decide whether the risks or the benefits have won out. There is always a risk that democracy will suffer, that citizens will have less access to their city government, that an increasing amount of public business will migrate to back rooms, and that big-city politics will begin to look like provincial and federal politics, from which Canadians feel increasingly excluded.

Municipal Political Parties

That sense of alienation could be abetted by the spread of party politics at the municipal level. Few cities in Canada have party politics, although two of the three large-city regions, Montreal and Vancouver, do. Unlike in the United States, where the Democrat and Republican parties operate at the national, state, and city levels, Canada's major political parties, the Liberals, Conservatives, and New Democrats, don't operate at the municipal level. Vancouver's civic politics have been dominated since 1940 by a centre-right party called the Non-Partisan Association (NPA). The NPA provided the mayor of Vancouver and won a plurality of the seats on city council 70 percent of the time since its establishment in 1940, when a fifty-four-year string of independent mayors was ended. The Vancouver electorate returned the NPA most of the time, only occasionally looking back to the ranks of independent candidates or to such centre-left parties as TEAM (The Electors' Action Movement) or COPE (the Coalition of Progressive Electors). In Montreal, a number of political parties have generally formed around the mayoral ambitions of an individual. The Montreal Island Citizens' Union is the vehicle for Mayor Gerald Tremblay, as Vision Montreal is the vehicle of his predecessor, Pierre Bourque. Like the Vancouver parties, they have a strong influence over the conduct of political campaigns and the processes of government.

But in other countries, municipal political parties are the norm. In the United States, they permeate every aspect of municipal life. Even municipal corporations that govern things like utilities and the running of elections are structured in a "bipartisan" way, to use that uniquely American word. Some, like the New York body that governs local elections, have a time-honoured tradition of swapping chairmen every term, so that one side will not be tempted to visit some devious plot on the other for fear of retribution. There are also municipal political parties in Sweden, Japan, Germany, and the UK.

Most practitioners of municipal government in Canada express a dislike for political parties. Their main objection, as with strong mayors, is that they harm democracy. Parties have several purposes. One is to extend a broad reach into the electorate and, through the articulation of policy and membership development, participate in creating a commodious tent, all of whose occupants are bent to the vital goal of electoral success. A second is for the development of policy. A third is for the discipline of governing, and it is this aspect that some people find troubling.

They point to the federal and provincial governments, dominated as they are by parties, and note how they've become increasingly exclusionary. Once an election campaign is concluded, parties retreat from view and carry on as much of their business as possible behind closed caucus doors. Particularly in governing parties, a tight tactical process is developed, one that schedules business, frames and articulates messages, limits spontaneous visibility, and controls potential damage. For safety's sake, everything is centralized, to be better controlled. And those on the fringes, or who resist being dominated, are left out, informed as little as possible about what is going on and subjected to party discipline such as the withholding of campaigning funds, plush appointments, and the various perks of the job. In a world where a slip of the tongue can have a devastating effect halfway round the world (think of Joe Clark's "What is the totality of your acreage?"), the fewer tongues the better.

This, of course, strikes at the very essence of representative democracy, and those who are used to city halls where, typically, citizens can address council and its committees face to face, find it lacking. In most cities, a citizen with something she wants to say can attend a council meeting and, during the time allotted for "deputations," have her say. And most council committees have open meetings with generous provision to hear from citizens. During discussions of property deals or personnel matters, meetings are closed so as to not taint the markets or violate privacy, but for the most part they are open. This makes for longer meetings and can complicate things. Critics generally dislike the messiness such a policy entails, arguing that it makes councils less efficient. They also don't like it when city councillors disagree with each other; they often look at the substantive disagreement two councillors might have, both of them adamant about the perfect rightness of their view, and wish they'd get on with it, that they'd stop letting the perfect be the enemy of the good. Ninety percent agreement is good enough, they say, and if they had a party they both belonged to, they'd quickly resolve their argument with 90 percent agreement, or the party leader would do it for them. And then the agenda could roll on, and the public business could proceed.

Defenders of City Hall's open democracy sometimes have a very romantic vision of that process. "Deputants" often have a different story to tell. It is a story of showing up at council with their passionate appeals, only to find that many councillors are absent, and most of the rest are doing paperwork, talking to one another or to their staffs, walking in and out during deputations, or are otherwise distracted. In addition, municipal staff in the room are often carrying on conversations with one another in normal speaking voices, even when within earshot of the deputant. Experienced deputants say that to succeed one must approach a councillor to champion the matter at hand, prepare arguments and talking points, and help line up other council support, all before showing up at council, so that when the council chair asks for response, a motion or referral can be quickly moved and passed. In other words, it should be lobbying as usual, as you would find it at any other level of government. Old hands will also tell you that there are loose affiliations of councillors who stick together on many, but not all, issues. And that there is a high degree of turf recognition, with each being ceded local mastery over her ward by the others. Both of these latter points mitigate democratic accessibility.

A vulnerable point for those defending party-free municipal government systems is the messiness. The presence of so many views, and so much nuance among them, can really slow things down. In smaller cities, or in the days when our present big cities were smaller, this may not have been a very expensive price to pay. But as cities have become bigger, both in population and area, the body of work before their governments has increased enormously. Infrastructure and services have grown from roads, curbs, and sidewalks to subways, wireless networks, and large-scale building-cooling systems. The arrival of tens of thousands of new residents per year has put planning and works departments under stress, forcing them to accelerate their approvals, in many cases reinventing their processes so as not to be swamped. Councils that once may have approved each development proposal now cannot give reasonable consideration to even a small fraction of them. But many councils have been reluctant to give up oversight of these matters, partly because they are dutiful, and partly because their approval is no small matter of control.

Part of the messiness comes from the fact that incentives in municipal governments are widely dispersed and various. What constitutes good government is a question with many answers. And the question of what constitutes a good and satisfying life for a councillor or mayor also has many answers. Each can consider and choose those answers that suit them best. One councillor might decide that being king or queen of the ward, a local somebody, is perfectly good enough, for now and into the long future. Another might decide that a grand city project bridging all the wards is worthy. Another might want to be mayor someday, and position herself accordingly. Another might unfortunately decide that there is money to be made by influencing what gets built where and by whom, and go on the take. Incentives tend to drive behaviour, and when incentives aren't aligned, behaviour can be all over the map.

Political parties align incentives. The party decides what is worth doing, and when and how it will be done. Those who wish to be successful align themselves with that, and the party sets about distributing the incentives. A seat to run in here, an appointment to a board or commission there, perhaps a "promotion" to run provincially or federally, or opportunities to hobnob with various political celebrities, all of these can be brought into play. And sometimes, when a government gets too comfortable, there might be contracts to be awarded for government work.

The greatest argument against parties is that undirected members of a council or legislature are free to argue the substance of issues and to differ with other views. By doing so they increase the understanding of public work and improve its quality. It is a quality that is seen in legislatures and parliaments that are loosely "whipped," where there are relatively few matters under discussion on which a government can fall from lack of confidence. Canada's parliaments are relatively heavily whipped, with a government's life hanging in the balance on most votes, so party members are advised to toe the line and to keep dissidence to a minimum. In the British and Indian parliaments, according to Queen's University parliamentary scholar C.E.S. Franks, members have more freedom to express their own views, with the result that some of them become quite expert in various fields, often writing books and delivering public commentaries. Excessive party discipline can dampen such intelligence.

But much depends on the rules. Heavy or light whipping of caucuses matters. Limiting the number of confidence votes, or the matters on which they can bring down a government (fiscal matters or senior appointments, for example) can free up debate. A polity can set the terms for the participation of parties, so that the benefits of debate, public inclusion, and diversity can be retained at the same time that the public business gets dealt with more effectively. Democracy is messy. Dictatorships can be much more streamlined, but eventually they tend to collapse in a grisly pile of rubble that takes a lot of time to sort through. As the Fram oil filter man said, you can pay me now or you can pay me later. In democracies that embrace citizen participation and inclusion, we pay a price in efficiency as we go along, but we tend to go along together, which prevents catastrophic collapses at the end of the day. It is the rules of that engagement that strike the balance between democratic government and effective government.

City-Wide or Ward Ridings?

Another key feature of city council operation is whether members are elected on a ward or city-wide basis. In Vancouver, members of council are elected city-wide. On the ballot, voters will find a list of all the mayoral and council candidates listed alphabetically. They can vote for one person for mayor, and for ten or fewer people for the ten council seats. The winners are the candidate for mayor who gets the most votes, and the top ten vote-getters for council. Whether you vote on Commercial Drive in the east end, around Little Mountain, in Kerrisdale in the west of the city, or in the west end near Stanley Park, you have the same ballot and candidates, all of whom hope to have broad appeal across the city if they are to win. Next to each name is their party affiliation, if they have one, which among other things is an aid to the inattentive, as it is in federal and provincial elections. Many of us don't know the players but cheer for the teams.

In the City of Ottawa, on the other hand, council candidates run in one of twenty-three wards across the city, and need only appeal to the voters of that ward. Only the candidates for mayor run city-wide. Every ward has a different ballot; only the section for mayoral candidates is the same across the city. Council candidates tend to stay within the wards during campaigns, going to where people congregate with messages about local concerns and issues. There is relatively little reward for expressing a broad vision of the city. And when they are elected, that parochialism can stay fixed—if not in anticipation of the next election, then out of loyalty to what worked. Most cities in Canada operate on the ward system.

Commentators tend to have two views on the merits of either system. If they are from a city without a ward system, they tend to see the merits of wards. If they are from a ward city, they tend to decry the parochialism it fosters, and yearn for a city-wide voting system that will produce broader visions. Enough with the potholes, speed bumps, snow removal, and raccoon fixations! Let's talk about attracting high-tech research facilities, waterfront redevelopment, and global trade!

There is, of course, something to be said for both approaches. A lively connection between a councillor and a part of the city is very useful, and, if the ratio of residents to councillor is low enough, people can have access to the councillor and let their views be known on an ongoing basis, not just through the ballot box at election time. Potholes, snow clearance (except in Vancouver and Victoria!), and raccoon control are important. How larger city initiatives will play out in the neighbourhoods is important, and a plugged-in councillor is a great conduit between local views and city actions. But councillors who are completely locally focused can ignore or minimize the larger possibilities that make cities grow and prosper, the connections to the world outside the city that can attract business, culture, and vigour. If they have no incentive to think outside their ward, they can become drags on progress.

Similarly, councillors without intimate ties to a part of the city can minimize the importance of the very local concerns that can add so tremendously to the quality of life. Neighbourhood parks need to be kept clean, functional, and attractive. Streets need to be safe and well maintained. Shopping streets need to be serviced and accessible. A city where council is not paying attention locally can let such things slip, often by underfunding the city agencies that service them. Annual budget balancing, a requirement provincial governments impose on cities, can snip away at the edges of department budgets, resulting in city swimming pools being closed or operating with reduced hours, corner trash bin pickup being cut back so that the bins are overflowing and smelly, and trees on main streets dying from lack of watering and care.

The grass is always greener in some other city's approach. Some people are beginning to talk about the merits of a hybrid system, with some members of a council elected on a ward system and others elected city-wide. Some countries, like New Zealand, have such a system, called "mixed-member," and where it is in use there are political parties involved—which, again, are aids to the inattentive. Municipal elections in Canada generally get lower turnouts than federal or provincial elections, and the notion that voters will keep track of who is who on the general list is doubtful. At the present time, they overwhelmingly vote for incumbents, even when those incumbents are remarkably and obviously unable. Better the fool we know than the fool we don't know. But we inevitably get the government we deserve, so not paying attention is not a good reason to avoid moving to a better system. It would be interesting for a large Canadian city to adopt a hybrid model, so that other cities could observe and learn.

Cities in Canada face enormous challenges, including finding the financing to deal with deferred maintenance on massive amounts of infrastructure, transit and transportation improvements, and amelioration of social inequity. They need strong and effective governments to find solutions and to work with other levels of government to both fund and coordinate responses. In many ways, their current government arrangements and approaches are inadequate to the challenges. They have to consider in a very serious way how they are going to improve their effectiveness. They need to look at creating a stronger executive authority in the mayor's office and with senior city staff, with appropriate council oversight mechanisms and protections. They need to be much more open to municipal political parties as a way of organizing local politics, and of creating more order in the conduct of public business, but with rules that protect public access to City Hall and council. And they need to look at the balance between very local and city-wide interests, and be prepared to structure themselves in a way that brings both views forward in a lively way. Strong or stronger mayors, municipal parties, and mixed-member councils should all be part of an active conversation about how we govern our cities.

7

STAND ON GUARD FOR THEE
Where Are the Leaders of Tomorrow?

Canada requires new and very different leadership if it is going to be able to liberate its big-city regions to serve the country better. It is a kind of leadership we are not used to seeing in this country. We are used to the bold, heroic kind of leadership, popularized in our entertainment culture and characterized by Pierre Trudeau's gunslinger pose and his "just watch me" rhetoric, or by Stephen Harper's lone-wolf bravado. Canadian leaders in recent decades have sought to gather power to them, to exclude that which they can't control, and to sully the views of their opponents. But it hasn't really worked very well.

There are other styles of leadership that aim to be less heroic, less wrapped up in personal attainment or achievement, and more enabling. They tend to styles of visionary leadership where the leader is not the centre or medium of the vision. They are not the norm in this country, but it is worth looking around to learn about other ways of leading, particularly ways that have worked. The last two decades have given us three instructive examples.

The Mexican Lesson

In the middle of Mexico City, that teeming, gritty, and throbbing metropolis, is a pine tree–covered hill where nestles a fine stone house for the president of Mexico. In the southwest corner of Chapultepec Park, the lungs and playground of the city's working class, Los Pinos has been the residence of Mexico's president since 1934. On a Monday in the spring of 1996, I entered the grounds of Los Pinos with a small group of Canadian business colleagues, and we were ushered beneath the pines and palms into a breakfast meeting with Ernesto Zedillo, president of Mexico.

Zedillo was a trim and fit-looking middle-aged man, a Mexican of European lineage. Like many leading figures in Mexico, he had been educated abroad, with a doctorate in economics from Yale University. With a reputation as somewhat of a technocrat, he had become a member of the dominant political party, the Partido Revolucionario Institucional (PRI), which had ruled Mexico and most of its states for seventy years. Under President Carlos Salinas (1988–94), Zedillo had served as secretary of budget and planning, and then secretary of public education. He resigned these positions to head up the presidential campaign for Luis Donaldo Colosio.

Under Mexico's constitution, presidents are limited to one six-year term. The PRI had established a protocol under which an outgoing president designated his successor. The PRI had established a lock on power by creating a seamless transition, as well as through entrenched corruption and intimidation that kept both voters and opposition politicians in line. The corruption had become so deep and venal that it had taken on a life of its own. Rather than corruption being an instrument of politics, politics had become an instrument of corruption. There were rumours of tight links to organized crime and the drug trade. Efforts at reform were met with either political stonewalling or violence. Legitimate businesses complained of being strong-armed by both thugs and politicians. People questioned where the PRI ended and the criminals began. It had reached the point where serious commentators, both internationally and within Mexico, were identifying the corruption as a principal barrier to Mexico's prosperity.

As the 1994 campaign was gearing up, Colosio was shot in the head at close range during a Tijuana campaign stop. Zedillo received Salinas's nod to replace Colosio and won the election.

Mexico and the world then turned to look at this relative unknown. Most expected more of the same, the brand of PRI insouciance about corruption and a closing of the ranks. Instead, they began to hear about economic and democratic reforms, the kind of talk they had heard from only the bravest of opposition politicians, and mostly in states remote from the capital. And they began to see actions based on that reform talk. The political system was opened up, justice reforms were initiated, a crackdown on drug trafficking was begun, and the economic reforms that Salinas had begun, primarily expressed in the terms of the North America Free Trade Agreement, were continued and deepened.

Losses in the 1997 state elections unsettled the party. Zedillo confirmed their worst fears in early 2000 by refusing to name his successor, as every PRI president had done before him. And when the election returns showed that the PRI candidate had been defeated by Vicente Fox of the Partido Acción Nacional, Zedillo conceded defeat quickly. Fearful that his party might refuse to relinquish the presidency, he conceded before anything could be cooked up.

Zedillo believed that Mexico had to change its political culture if it was going to be a country of the future. It had to drop its feudal past and embrace modern, networked economics characterized by Mexicans looking outwards to the world for markets, lessons, and technologies. That meant, among other things, more open politics that could trade in different ideas and approaches, and involve different people. He knew that, at least symbolically, the grip of the PRI had to be loosened, if not broken. And he knew that if he did that, Mexico would benefit, but he would not. He would be *persona non grata* with party old-liners, as he was becoming with the historic partners in corruption. He would not enjoy a lavish retirement in the mansions in the hills above Mexico City, approval in the dining rooms of the country clubs, or an easy ride in the circles of privilege.

US president Bill Clinton, whose term coincided with Zedillo's, characterized his conduct as "one of the great acts of statesmanship in the history of modern democracy." At the centre of that act was an ability to relinquish power, both personally and for his political colleagues, who were bound to be displeased, and were.

Los Pinos on that spring morning was a soothing and enticing place, wind whispering in the pine and palm leaves, the air fragrant with their perfume, and the grounds offering a peaceful respite from the struggles and tensions of a country trying to make its future. It would have been a comfortable place to stay and do business as usual, as had many before him.

Zedillo would have known, though, that statesmanship was in the air. He would have seen the power of "less is more" reshaping Europe and South Africa.

Gorbachev and the USSR

He would have seen it in the Union of Soviet Socialist Republics from 1985, when Mikhail Gorbachev became the general secretary of the Communist Party and head of the government. He succeeded the long and grim reign of Leonid Brezhnev, and the short terms of the nasty Yuri Andropov and the ineffective Konstantin Chernenko. The USSR had been through a long nightmare under the brutal Josef Stalin, the buffoonish but stealthily liberalizing Nikita Khrushchev, and the hard-nosed Brezhnev. Devastated economically after World War II, there was a period of economic revival under Khrushchev, but things had been going downhill for some time. The Cold War had taken its toll in diverting resources to military ends.

Gorbachev knew things had to change, and in a sprawling and complex place like the USSR, which patched together a wide-ranging and diverse set of republics, he must have known that change would be a wild ride. Historian Michael Beschloss once noted that "there is not an ounce of subtlety between Vilnius and Vladivostok." Gorbachev began by talking about two new policies. *Glasnost* would be an opening up of life, first with increased freedom of speech and fewer controls on the press. *Perestroika* was a reconstruction of the economy, with the intention of ending tight state control of all enterprise. The reforms were generally unsuccessful, and led to unrest as the economy stumbled and the constituent republics became volatile. Still, Gorbachev pressed on with reforms, despite severe political pressure. It was clear that he saw the way forward leading to more democracy, more economic freedom, and more individual freedom. Perhaps inevitably, the USSR collapsed in a dramatic scene that looked like a *coup d'état*, complete with fleeing elites under arrest in their vacation houses.

The old saw has it that "if it ain't broke, don't fix it." Gorbachev obviously thought the USSR was broken, and that it needed fixing, and if he didn't get to work it might be too late. A career man in the rough Soviet political world, he was probably not greatly surprised at the chaos his reforms created, nor that he became one of its victims. He must have sensed the personal risks he was animating, but thought that it was his greatest duty to history, and to the future of his people.

De Klerk in South Africa

An observer of these events from another hemisphere must have been Frederik Willem de Klerk of South Africa. A lawyer first elected to Parliament in 1969, at the age of thirty-three, he became a stalwart on the front benches of the National Party, the dominant political force in apartheid South Africa. Late in his cabinet career, he became a leading member of the reformist wing of the NP, and was elected party leader and president in 1989.

Apartheid was the overwhelming historic fact of South Africa. A glaring abuse of human rights, the suppression of non-whites ostracized the country from the company of civilized nations. But even the approbation of the rest of the world did not budge the obstinate Boer-dominated political world, which rebuffed foreign appeals for reform and brutally suppressed internal efforts. The symbol of the repressed was the leader of the Africa National Congress, Nelson Mandela. A lawyer and seemingly fearless campaigner for the defeat of apartheid, Mandela was arrested and imprisoned in primitive conditions. South African prime ministers and governments remained impervious to any appeals for Mandela's release, no matter which president, prime minister, king, or queen called for it, no matter what argument was made. Keeping him in prison became a symbol of undisputable power.

Part of the white population wanted apartheid to end, because they could see what their isolation in the world was doing to the country that was blessed by nature in so many ways and that boasted the most successful economy in Africa. But they all feared the aftermath, the removal of the brutally repressive lid that had kept the blacks down. These were de Klerk's people, the stalwarts of the National Party. They were the people with whom he'd grown up, gone to law school, sat in Cabinet, and relied on to make him prime minister. Some of them were adamant supporters of apartheid; many others were not supporters, but were fearful of the results of ending it. Some felt strongly the effects of international condemnation, particularly the business and investment bans that were mounting by the year. In 1961, South Africa had been excluded from the British Commonwealth, and in 1962 it had been condemned by the United Nations. The sharpest rebuke for sports-mad white South Africans was the exclusion of their teams from international competition, as nation after nation refused to play them. This was a great blow to their rugby union supporters, who long believed that the Springboks, the national team, was the world's best, and whose confrontations with the New Zealand All-Blacks were the stuff of legend.

When de Klerk became president in 1989, he could have tried to ride out the increasingly uncomfortable policy of apartheid, mollifying some anti-apartheid sentiment through slow reforms.

Instead, in his first major speech as president on February 2, 1990, he lifted the ban on the principal political parties of black South Africans and outlined his intention to create a non-racist country. Nine days later he released Mandela from prison. On that summer Sunday afternoon, Mandela was a free man for the first time in twenty-seven years, and South Africa was set irrevocably on a road of change. In 1993, Mandela and de Klerk were jointly awarded the Nobel Peace Prize. At the ceremony in Oslo, de Klerk noted that the two were receiving the Nobel together, and shortly would embark on a political campaign against each other. That this could be done with relative equanimity was a sign of immense progress for their country. The ANC won the campaign, and in 1994 Mandela became president.

De Klerk must have known the inevitability of his defeat. He could do the arithmetic, in a country where blacks outnumber whites 8–1. Mandela proved a charismatic and effective leader, both at home and abroad. A key turning point occurred in 1995, when the rugby World Cup was held in South Africa. Primarily a game of the white elites, rugby was not popular with blacks, and the Springboks were particularly disliked. South Africa won the tournament with a thrilling last-minute score, and during the presentation ceremony Mandela appeared on the field of the stadium wearing a Springbok jersey, beaming with pleasure, leading the celebrations. He presented the victor's trophy to Springbok captain Francois Pienaar, an Afrikaner, and pictures of the two men united in joy were flashed across the country and around the world. A corner was turned for the country, and the process of reconciliation between the races was inalterable from that moment on. Bumpy, but sure.

De Klerk largely faded from view. He had some health problems and a public divorce, and made speeches abroad from time to time, but was never again a national figure. He lost a great deal by his actions.

■ ■ ■

These three leaders are united by their actions of relinquishing power. Their motives were always complicated and mixed, and each probably thought at some point that there was a way for them to ride out the storms of change. Zedillo, of course, knew his exit was determined by Mexico's constitution, and perhaps Gorbachev and de Klerk knew that life at the top of their volatile political societies would be short-lived. Maybe they all thought things would work out, but even when things began to go sideways for them, they kept pursuing the reforms that they knew were better for their country, even if the aftermath didn't turn out too well for them and their political colleagues.

In *Nineteen Eighty-Four*, George Orwell has one character tell another that "power is not a means, it is an end." In most political cultures, this seems to be the rule. These three men broke the rule, and paid a price. Not a desperate price, not their lives or penury, which others have suffered over history. But they made a choice within the systems of their countries that placed the good of the countries first.

In Canada, we do not live in such dramatic times. But we do have political systems and politicians who focus on power as an end. And if we are to empower our big-city regions for the good of the nation, we need to find those politicians who are prepared to relinquish power, to see their power transferred to other leaders for other purposes.

"Senior" Governments and Cities

In a speech in 1967, Prime Minister Lester Pearson said, "Urbanization with all its problems has become the dominant social and economic condition of Canadian life." Noting problems of housing, traffic, pollution, poverty, and sprawl, he identified the lack of sufficient tax revenues and the blurred accountability between levels of government as sources of the problems that were being created. But he left office the next year. The federal government of Pierre Trudeau established a ministry of state for urban affairs, a not quite fully fledged department headed by a not quite fully fledged minister. Successively, Robert Andras, Ron Basford, Barney Danson, and André Ouellet headed a ministry with no programs and no funds. It was established in 1971 and disbanded at the end of March in 1979, and attempted to animate a tri-level process of dealing with the new urban reality. But it foundered on provincial resistance to federal intrusion in municipal affairs. The provinces feared it was an attempt of the federal government to dilute the importance of the federal-provincial relationship. Ever since, federal governments have been reluctant to engage the cities, with the exception of Paul Martin's mostly rhetorical excursion. More typical have been the firm expressions of Jean Chrétien and Stephen Harper that cities are provincial responsibilities.

After World War II, the federal Central Mortgage and Housing Corporation had direct relations with many municipalities. The CMHC was a Crown corporation that acted like a bank for the assembly and preparation of land for housing and related development, and eventually broadened its mandate to include planning and infrastructure development. The provinces tolerated Ottawa's involvement because it had financial capacity beyond their own, financing 75 percent to the province's 25 percent, and because Ottawa allowed them a fair amount of control over projects in their jurisdiction. While CMHC (renamed in 1979 the Canada Mortgage and Housing Corporation) remains the second-largest Crown corporation (after Canada Post), in recent decades it has withdrawn from direct involvement in planning and building housing as governments have vainly looked to the market to provide low-income housing.

Canadian mayors have come and gone on these issues. A usual trajectory is to see a newly elected mayor, bright-eyed and bushy-tailed, with all sorts of wonderful ideas about how they will make deals with the federal and provincial governments, because they have "a plan." And they are only too happy to take you through that plan, which mainly involves a statement of need, which is real, and which they find terribly persuasive. Their expectation is that the federal or provincial government will look at the plan, be stricken by its value, and arrange to transfer the funds and authority for the mayor to enact the plan. A year or two later, that same mayor is dull-eyed and the tail is dragging, and the plan is in tatters. They have run up against the power wall, and can't find a way up it or around it. It makes some mayors more resourceful and less ambitious, it makes others mad, and it reduces some, like former Toronto mayor Mel Lastman, to name-calling.

What most of them find so disappointing is the lack of recognition at the federal and provincial levels for the bind in which they find themselves. They have growing responsibilities and obligations on one hand, as cities get bigger and more complex, while on the other they face constrained revenues that are locked into a primary revenue source that doesn't grow with the economy. The mayors look at other developed countries, the ones with which Canada competes in the world economy, and see that they have national programs to fund assisted and low-income housing, public transit systems, and infrastructure, but that Canada doesn't. They see cities in other countries with access to taxes—such as income and sales taxes—that grow with the economy, that Canadian cities lack. They see other large cities being able to use debt and debt-like instruments to finance growth, but Canadian cities are required to balance their budgets annually. So, they wonder, what gives?

They wonder why the other levels of government aren't more interested in or attentive to cities. One reason is the unequal distribution of votes in Canada, which favours non-urban regions. The average rural riding has about 85,000 voters, versus 120,000 in the average urban riding, so Parliament hears rural voices disproportionately. Part of the reason is a lag in redrawing the constituency lines as urban regions grow. Part of it is a deliberate policy to make sure the rural voice is not overwhelmed.

Another reason is the political boss system used by parties, where one member is given special responsibility for a region, and the quality of the relationship depends very much on that person. Often, that person treats the region like a fiefdom. What he doesn't like doesn't go forward, so seemingly sensible projects that have broad appeal find themselves facing either a roadblock—or at least a speed bump. During the government of Paul Martin, Toronto MP Joe Volpe was the designated minister with responsibility for Toronto, and the federal government's lack of engagement with the city on such issues as waterfront development, transit, or public-housing redevelopment puzzled many people. One rumour that circulated hinted that Volpe didn't like Mayor David Miller's political allegiance to the New Democratic Party, and was letting that serve as a barrier to progress. True or not, it was entirely believable and not unlikely in a system where the lack of systemic engagement between the city and the federal government forced matters into narrow channels.

As disappointing as their periodic supplications to provincial and federal governments have been, mayors have never stopped trying. Sometimes they succeed, as Vancouver's Philip Owen did in securing the innovative Four Pillars Drug Strategy program for the drug-addicted population in his city's lower east side. As often as not, the results are slow and meagre. The problem is that separate negotiations have to take place on every deal, starting from scratch. This is what happens when you have to ask permission each time. Such one-by-one deal-making takes time and energy and limits the amount that can be achieved because of the limits on time and energy available.

The framework needs to change, and that is what the de Klerks, Zedillos, and Gorbachevs of the world figured out. They had to change the way things operated to create the enabling environment for change and progress.

In Canada, few politicians get it. Some people thought Paul Martin did when he talked about the importance of cities and made some infrastructure funding available out of the federal gas tax revenues. But he didn't change the nature of the game at all. He required the cities to submit proposals for a share of the money, and these had to be in accord with his government's ideas of what should be done in order to qualify. There is something irresistible about holding the purse strings, and almost nobody wants to let them go. From the taxpayer's point of view, there is only one tax dollar and it gets split between the

federal, provincial, and municipal governments (municipal governments get only eight cents out of each tax dollar). It should be split on
the basis of the relative needs of governments to provide the programs
and services Canadians need and want. But governments develop very
proprietary attitudes about the money they take in, coming to view it
as "their" money. Many people have commented on feeling a sense
of astonishment after hearing a provincial or federal politician or
bureaucrat ask, "Why should we give them some of our money?"

Signs of Hope

A politician who shows some signs of understanding that things need
to change is Ontario premier Dalton McGuinty. A much underrated
premier, McGuinty listens and learns. In the early 2000s, as leader of
the Opposition, he was briefed by Jane Jacobs, Conference Board of
Canada president Anne Golden, former Toronto mayor Barbara Hall,
and others on the place of cities in Canada. And he had a number of
naive and untutored questions to ask. By the time of a second briefing
a few months later, he had absorbed a lot of what he heard, and had
smart and probing questions. Four years later, as premier, he introduced a revised City of Toronto Act that began to make some fundamental changes to the relationship between the province and the city.
Over the resistance of others in his government, McGuinty champi-
oned the changes, which effectively began to shift more powers and
authority from the province. The previous law had been prescriptive:
if it is not in the Act, you either can't do it or have to seek permission.
The revised Act was permissive: if it is in the Act, you have to do it, but
if it isn't in the act, you can make your own decision. And, significantly, under the new Act the province must be able to show a clear
provincial interest to justify its interventions, while the city has the
right to resort to the courts to resolve disputes. The revised Act is far

from perfect. It doesn't deal with finance and fiscal issues in a way that is sufficiently empowering; although it does allow for the levying of some excise taxes municipally, it excludes the two big material taxes: income and sales. And it still leaves with the province the power to change the relationship unilaterally. A future provincial government could repeal the Act and impose something much more prescriptive. But McGuinty has begun a journey down the right road, and it will be harder for a future government to backtrack—there will be a much higher political price to pay. McGuinty was re-elected in October 2007 with a thumping majority, in part a tribute to the period of very good government he had produced for Ontario.

In British Columbia, Premier Gordon Campbell, a former Vancouver mayor, has also shown some desire to change the relationship. His BC Community Charter contains key elements that empower municipalities. First, it recognizes them as an "order of government," as are the provincial and federal governments. It talks about the importance of each level of government respecting the authority and "turf" of the other, and it recognizes the principle that the province should not saddle the cities with obligations without ensuring that they have the access to financial resources to pay for them. Critics of Campbell's Community Charter doubt its sincerity, claiming it merely sets the table for an offloading of provincial obligations to the cities as a way of removing costs from the provincial budget. After all, they note, this is exactly what Mike Harris did in Ontario, to disastrous effect, although Harris still failed to balance his budgets.

There are some places in Canada where provincial and federal governments share their tax revenues with cities. Paul Martin's government shared some of its portion of the gasoline tax with cities, a total of $5 billion over five years, but only for projects that met with federal government approval. And Ottawa made unconditional rebates of the

Goods and Services Tax, the federal sales tax, paid out by cities. In Manitoba, the provincial government shares 2 percent of its personal income tax revenue and 1 percent of its corporate income tax revenue with cities. In British Columbia, the provincial government lets Translink, the Greater Vancouver transit and transportation authority, levy an eleven-cent-per-litre gasoline tax. Montreal receives revenue from a 1.5-cent-per-litre gas tax from the province, while Edmonton and Calgary also receive fuel-tax revenue from Alberta. In each of these cases, the cities' access to this money could be terminated arbitrarily by the government that has extended the largesse to them. They have been granted a benefit, but they do not possess a right.

Old Habits Die Hard

In this regard they are like any intergovernmental transfers to cities. All of the power resides with the government that has the right and ability to tax, and to distribute the tax revenues. To tax is to govern. And that power is very appealing.

The public rhetoric related to empowering cities is revealing. Stephen Harper's Finance minister, Jim Flaherty, himself a former provincial finance minister, has resisted a federal funding role for cities with the admonition that cities should "get their houses in order." A similar piece of advice has come from former Ontario Finance minister Greg Sorbara in the McGuinty government.

But private rhetoric is even worse: members of federal and provincial governments regard municipal politicians as bumpkins—unsophisticated and undisciplined hicks. Civil servants are often dismissive of their municipal counterparts, regarding them as pothole fillers and garbage collectors.

The bases for these views are insubstantial, for the most part. As has been discussed elsewhere, the lack of party organization at the municipal level often makes the practice of democracy look messy. But city governments operate their basic infrastructure and human services in a way that is admired around the world. And provincial and federal governments seem surprisingly prone to forget the report cards of their auditors general as they excoriate the performance of their city cousins.

The rhetoric is likely rooted in the urge to defend power. Once a city is given the power to levy income and sales taxes, and set the levels of those taxes, it is unlikely that it could be taken away from them. Once they have the revenues that allow them to control their destiny, there is a strong possibility that a better-served citizenry will accept the rationale that it is better to pay the city than the province. And if the city were to take over the funding of its own health and education systems, the two big public expenditures, and do a better job of it because of their greater understanding of local needs and conditions, people might wonder what good the province was. In a relatively short time, both identification with and allegiance to the province might dwindle, and an effective city-state might emerge—a city-state where the power and glory of the mayor might easily eclipse that of the premier of the province.

That is not why people want to become premiers of provinces. Politicians need robust egos to be able to put up with the slings and arrows of political life. They know they can always count on an opponent to work at bringing them down. The last instinct they have is to bring themselves down.

At the same time, the better politicians are in public life to make things better, to improve the life of our communities and country. Cynical observers doubt this, but generally people who get to the top of our political world could be making more money and having better lives elsewhere. It might not be quite as exciting. As former Ontario premier David Peterson said, "The dullest day in politics is equal to the best day on Bay Street." But former New York governor Mario Cuomo captured it best in an interview a few years after he left office. He was asked what he missed the most, and the interviewer admitted that he was thinking of the lifestyle or the power, but Cuomo answered that he missed going out every day and putting his shoulder to the stone. Some days, he said, we moved it up a bit, and some days it slipped back, but it was the fact that we had our shoulder to the stone that counted.

This is the kind of politician that might be able to break the deadlock of Canada's governmental arrangements, that might begin to redistribute power in such a way as to let our large cities begin to find their destiny. Is it a Dalton McGuinty building on his first-term reforms, deepening them and letting the big cities in the province climb to their feet? Is it Gordon Campbell in British Columbia, declaring that his Community Charter was indeed a blueprint, and that he was now going to take steps to give the great population of the Lower Mainland its wings? Will it be a smart and politically sophisticated mayor like Gerald Tremblay in Montreal, who will find new ways to work in the complex politics of Quebec to untie the strings to the provincial capital?

Or will it be Stephen Harper, or Stéphane Dion, or a future prime minister who looks at what the country needs to do to capitalize on the huge underperforming asset of the big-city regions and says, "I know what the Constitution says, and what tradition dictates, but I can see a better future for Canada, and I will do whatever it takes to make it happen"?

8

KEEP OUR LAND
Small Steps That Will Work Now

Canada sometimes seems like a country preserved in amber. For those interested in change, it seems like a hard place to make it. Our constitutional structure exerts a drag on modernizing our practice.

There have been times when we were able to make change in Canada. Jack Granatstein outlines such a period in his terrific book *The Ottawa Men*, which chronicles the rise of the federal public service and its golden age. The book traces the lives and contributions of such men as O.D. Skelton, Norman Robertson, Clifford Clark, Bill Macintosh, and John Deutsch, who built the modern public service and put in place many of the basic programs that created the springboard for prosperity. The other great period was between 1960 and 1975, when medicare and equalization programs were developed. Today, given regional differences, it would be difficult to embark upon such grand projects.

But we have what we have, and we live with it. The failed attempts to change the Constitution in the 1980s at Charlottetown and Meech Lake have locked that mechanism away for a generation or more. As Senator Hugh Segal has commented, the country serves the

Constitution rather than the Constitution serving the country. Any change will have to be accomplished without formal change to our organizing documents. We will have to change the arrangements, without changing the law. It is like rearranging the furniture without touching the floor, walls, or ceiling.

The good news is that a lot can be achieved this way. It is often hard fought, hard won, and enervating, but change can occur. In the last three decades, powers have flowed from the federal government to the provinces, especially to Quebec, without changing the Constitution. The First Nations have gained elements of self-government. Most of this movement has involved a transfer of powers or money from the federal to provincial governments, all relatively seamlessly. The steps have not been big, or bold, and have seemed like a series of baby steps—small enough to keep from toppling, but frequent enough to move forward slowly.

How the Federal Government Can Help Cities

We all know that much has changed over the last 150 years—not least the growth in the importance of cities. In 1867, when Sir John A. Macdonald and his colleagues were creating Canada, it is clear that they intended to place the big matters of government in the hands of the federal government. Had they known how important some issues—such as education and health care—would become, it may be argued that they would have placed them at the federal level. At the time, however, they were not considered to be critical state functions at all, and therefore became provincial responsibilities. As did municipalities.

What might be some of the ways the federal government, the level constitutionally barred from direct involvement in cities, can contribute to them? While cities are the creatures of the provinces, the federal government can intervene in two ways: through intermediaries, or by directly funding people. For example, the federal government in the 1990s funded environmental initiatives in cities by channelling the money through the Federation of Canadian Municipalities (FCM). And the federal government engaged in funding universities, another provincial jurisdiction, by awarding Millennium Scholarships directly to students. Both of these approaches offer a way for the federal government to support cities. Such direct funding can be done—like scholarships or rent supplements—by giving grants to individuals, or through the tax system, by giving tax credits or benefits.

Of course, Ottawa could choose to do it in such a way as to fulfill a federal government mandate (a prescriptive approach), or it could support a city agenda (an enabling approach). Examples abound of the prescriptive approach, as discussed earlier in relation to the Martin government's gas tax money, which was used to create a contest among cities to see which could best put federal priorities into practice. But a more enabling approach would listen to the needs of the cities and design responses. It would listen to the collective needs, as expressed through associations like the FCM, but it would also listen to individual cities, because they have unique needs that require unique solutions. Some cities need subways, some light rail, some bus-ways, some suburban rail commuter lines, and some jitney buses. Some need housing for new immigrants, some for aging farmers moving to town.

The federal government is not there to attend to every city need, clearly. Yet there are matters of significant importance to country building to which it should pay attention. By contributing to a stable economic platform or to the development of internationally competitive human capital, virtually every country in the developed world has a national housing policy and program and a national transportation policy and program; and because most people live in cities, these programs are largely urban in scope. Canada has neither.

We used to have both. After World War II, we had a national housing policy, which began with the goal of housing returning soldiers, then broadened into a more general set of programs aimed at providing good-quality housing for the working class. The Central Mortgage and Housing Corporation, subsequently renamed the Canada Housing and Mortgage Corporation, not only provided and facilitated financing, it established a building code to improve quality. CMHC became the provider of subsidies that allowed low-income housing to be provided for the poor, as well as assisted housing for those with disabilities. The provinces allowed these intrusions into city development because there was federal money to be had, and because, after it set the standards, CMHC left a lot of power in provincial hands.

We also had a transportation policy after the war, one centred on automobiles and roads. The government financed roads, and attracted automotive production by creating an enabling regulatory environment through the Auto Pact and related tariff concessions on car parts. The federal government also funded the capital programs of transit systems, assisting them to buy subway cars, buses, and streetcars.

But that active hand has been drawn back. Housing policy, both in terms of creativity and financial clout, is a shadow of its former self, and any transportation policy that exists is still focused on roads and cars, with only sporadic nods in the direction of urban transit systems.

If the federal government were to look at three big issues that relate to country-building, to the creation of a sound economic climate and a fertile social climate, it might focus on the issues of transit, housing, and immigrant settlement. The ability of people to move easily and in a timely way across the region provides a mobile and flexible workforce, and it allows consumers to move easily to a point of sale, to buy a screwdriver, mortgage, or opera ticket. Housing people in safe and affordable homes provides a stable platform for work, achievement in school, and social engagement. And the rapid and effective settlement of immigrants, particularly their ability to find the employment for which they have been trained and have experience, makes them quicker contributors to the economy and society, which therefore enhances our international outreach and competitiveness.

How might the federal government engage in these issues?

Urban Transit Needs Funding Help

To support urban transit systems, the government could make transit passes tax-deductible. Passes provided by corporations to employees could be a business expense, or in the case of a pass purchased directly by an individual, she could claim it as a tax deduction. This would encourage the purchase of transit passes, and would increase ridership and boost revenues. Those revenues could be applied to improving the system, making it more appealing and convenient. Transit system operators say that such stimulation creates a virtuous circle: the better a system gets, the more people want to use it, which generates the revenues to improve facilities and service. Increased revenues can lead to more frequent service, as transit systems either put more buses and streetcars on the road or build dedicated transit corridors, as Ottawa and Calgary have done with their busways, or as Toronto has done with dedicated streetcar lines along St. Clair and Spadina avenues, with ambitious plans to extend them across the city. Or transit operators could install customer-friendly amenities like those found in Stockholm and Amsterdam and at Vancouver's Seabus terminals, where a digital clock tells you when the next vehicle will arrive. In Vancouver, if a commuter sees that the next ferry leaves in ten minutes, she may detour to pick up a coffee or snack to take aboard, which boosts the revenues of the retailers in the station, allowing the landlord, often the public transit authority, to raise the rents. A virtuous circle.

Public transit systems in Canadian cities require external funding. The Toronto Transit Commission is the most successful in North America at meeting costs from the fare box. The TTC gets about 80 percent of its operating costs from fares. The next most successful is New York City, at half of Toronto's rate. Most get less than a quarter as much as Toronto from the fare box. And this only accounts for operating costs, and does not include the capital costs of new vehicles, equipment, and constructing new routes. For this capital, transit systems have to look elsewhere. And the costs of equipment have been increasing rapidly in recent years. Streetcars that used to cost a few hundred thousand dollars now cost several million. Typically, Canadian transit systems cover their capital budgets by way of grants from the provincial or federal governments. How much they get depends on the fiscal condition of the granting government, and on whether that government agrees with the expenditure. Sometimes they foist their own projects on the city and its transit system, against best advice and at great cost locally through the obligations associated with shared-cost local funding, as happened in Toronto with the construction of the Sheppard subway line.

In other jurisdictions around the world, a common way to build a new transit route, or to purchase new vehicles and equipment, is to issue a municipal bond. The bonds are sold to the public, at competitive rates, and the interest and principal repayments are backed in part by the anticipated fares from the existing or new service, and in part by charges levied against new development related to the new or improved transit line. Sinking funds are put in place in order to ensure that the annual interest payments can be made and that the big lump-sum principal repayment can be made at the end of the bond's term. These sinking funds are created by allocating a portion of annual revenues to them, as they might also be allocated to a reserve or contingency fund. This mechanism, and its sister, tax increment financing, makes available a large sum of money up front, to be repaid over a long period of time. But it requires stability both of anticipated revenue and of political conditions.

In Canada, municipal transit companies don't enjoy the same liberty to issue bonds, or the resources to create large sinking funds. The federal and provincial governments could help. They could permit the issuance of municipal bonds or transit bonds. They could either guarantee interest and principal repayment, or guarantee that any shortfall in annual revenue that would shortchange a sinking fund would be made up. In effect, they could create the financial stability to make such financing possible.

And, to sweeten the deal, they could make them tax-free bonds, so that interest payments would not be taxable.

Closing the Low-Income Housing Gap

Housing is an ongoing issue, particularly in growing cities, which typically are the larger cities. While the market tends to take care of most income segments, it does not provide low-income housing, which is housing for the chronically poor or those entering the ownership market for the first time. Due to the same construction dynamics, it does not provide sufficient rental housing. While there is a general preference for home ownership, because of its contribution to stability and asset building, many people either do not want to own, or may not be ready to own, so renting is a better solution for them. But the market has not been producing an adequate supply of rental housing. Nor does the market meet the needs of those who require assisted housing—who regularly need some attention or supervision because of a disability.

Low-income housing is a hard nut to crack. Numerous people of good will have tried to crack it over the years, but they keep running up against some inevitable arithmetic. The basic problem is a gap of at least 25 percent between what it costs to build a unit of housing and what someone on a low income can afford to pay for it. In the past in Canada, as in other places, governments used to fill that gap. As mentioned above, CMHC used to subsidize the building of housing, first for returning soldiers and then for the burgeoning middle class. Now nobody but the odd charity or sporadic government program does, and so there is a hole at the bottom of the market. Laird Hunter, an Edmonton lawyer familiar with housing, calls this hole a case of "market failure."

There are two ways to deal with it: revive a program of public subsidies, for only the public sector can do it at sufficient scale to make a dent in the problem; or reduce the cost of housing. The latter is possible, and such innovations as the Grow Home by Avi Friedman of McGill University, or various designs for "incremental" houses by Toronto architect John van Nostrand, show how. But in most parts of Canada, the actual costs of building are almost matched by such things as taxes, development fees, levies to support school boards, and other items that provide revenues that the recipients are loathe to surrender. So even if Friedman or van Nostrand could develop Grow Home or incremental housing at scale, all the other levies would keep the prices elevated just beyond the reach of low-income people. Another approach advocated by people like Toronto architect Margie Zeidler is the refurbishment of old buildings, which can be done at a cost per unit well below that of new construction, reaching closer to low incomes. Zeidler has shown how that approach can provide office space to people and groups who can't afford high rents in her two admirable Toronto buildings known by their addresses, 401 Richmond and 215 Spadina. In that same city, social entrepreneur Susan Pigott is spearheading an effort to acquire a set of apartment buildings in South Parkdale that may become gentrified in a few years. The area is home to a great stock of aging low-income apartment buildings that need refurbishment. They may either be modestly renovated and kept, at least in part, as low-income rental units, or more lavishly redone and sold as condominium units. Pigott realizes that it is a moment in time to preserve housing within reach of low-income people, and not allow them to be forced to the cheaper fringes of the city. In Vancouver in 2007, the provincial government bought ten old hotel/apartment buildings with the intention of renovating them and keeping them available to low-income tenants. In doing so, it accelerated the city government's ten-year plan to such an extent that Mayor Sam Sullivan was able to announce "mission accomplished."

Every little bit helps, so housing advocates have recommended a suite of initiatives that could chip away at the cost of developing low-income housing. The "silver bullet" is government realizing how critical it is to participate with substantial subsidies, but after several decades advocates have stopped holding their breath on that possibility, despite the occasional and sporadic efforts such as the one BC premier Gordon Campbell made for Vancouver. Instead, they have embraced the approach of many small things rather than one big thing.

For example, they have recommended that builders of low-income rental housing be able to roll over their capital gains into new low-income rental projects without paying capital gains tax on them. So, if the developer of a project made $1 million, she would have to pay a capital gains tax of about $250,000. But if her intention was to invest that gain into a new project, and she didn't have to pay that quarter-million dollars in tax, she could put the full million into the new project rather than only $750,000. This would significantly increase the amount of money going into low-income housing. The government would collect its capital gains tax at the point that the developer decided not to do another project, or when there was a significant gap between projects.

It would also be helpful if that same developer could accelerate the depreciation of the project, additionally reducing the tax burden. But this should only be permitted on reinvestment in a new low-income project.

The rebate of the Goods and Services Tax would also benefit such projects, and reduce significantly the cost of building.

Ottawa Dealing Directly with Canadians

One of the best ideas to bolster the production of affordable housing has come from Tom Kent, one of the greatest social policy minds in Canada's history. Kent, a former assistant editor of *The Economist* and advisor to prime ministers Pearson and Trudeau, has a comprehensive grasp of both the substance and the instruments of policy, and can always find the right tool for the job. He recommends the creation of a refundable tax credit for rental or mortgage payments, aimed at subsidizing market rents for low-income Canadians. For people who do not have enough income to be required to pay tax, the refundable tax credit would result in a payment to them by the government to subsidize their ability to make rent or mortgage payments. This has an advantage of being income tested, so the benefit is not extended to those who do not need it.

Such a proposal is tantamount to a guaranteed income or a negative income tax, and is often a hard sell, because it can be seen as pampering poor people or as a disincentive to work. These views are usually held by those on the right of the political spectrum and derided for their lack of "common sense," a phrase that seems to have been hijacked from its traditional meaning. It used to mean something so well investigated and understood that it has passed into the common consciousness as a given. It now means something so blindingly obvious that it does not need further investigation, like the obduracy and inevitability of the poor. However, further investigation of low-income people reveals discomfiting details; for instance, about half the people on welfare in Canada have a disability, and many of the rest are widowed seniors and single mothers. There is also a high correlation between poverty and many negative social outcomes, like illiteracy, poor health, brushes with the law, and poor academic performance. One of the critical factors in poverty is unstable housing; being forced by the rental market to move frequently disrupts a parent's ability to keep a job and a child's attachment to a school and schoolmates. Stabilizing housing is a critical factor in stabilizing lives. There are relatively few chronic poor in Canada, but a distressingly high number are on the margins—in a position to move in and out of poverty many times in their life, always one piece of bad luck or one bad decision away from losing their assets and their home. A proposal such as Tom Kent's can provide a critical tool for the stabilization of lives. And for cities it can provide a needed boost to the affordable housing market and create a mini-boom in construction and renovation.

Another way to stimulate cities would be an elaboration of the Millennium Scholarship Fund, the program implemented by Jean Chrétien's government to make it easier for good, well-rounded students to go to Canadian universities or colleges, and for the country to retain good young people who otherwise might follow scholarships to universities in other countries. The federal government—or a provincial government, for that matter—might establish a scholarship program for bright and accomplished students from outside Canada, predominantly in the developing world, to come to Canadian universities. The scholarship should be generous enough to cover tuition and related education costs, living expenses, and periodic travel home during the course of their undergraduate degree. The program should be comprehensive, not just bringing a student here to fend for themselves, but providing them with faculty advisors, community mentors, and a network of peers. The program might easily be managed by groups external to government, like the excellent Canadian Merit Scholarship Foundation, which already runs a similar program for Canadian students.

Such a program would have numerous benefits. It would clearly help the student who might find opportunities for education blocked by lack of finances, inadequate institutions in her home country, or societal norms. It would benefit Canada by attracting a bright and diverse cadre of wonderful young people, some of whom would stay when their education was finished, and all of whom would retain networks that could nourish Canada economically, culturally, and socially. This is based on another great idea of Kent's, that Canada's immigration policy should be focused on young people who can bring a lifetime of high-level contribution with them. Of course, there should be a concern about stripping other countries of their brightest youth, but is it right to restrict opportunity for others unilaterally? Should not the decision be theirs, once they have considered the opportunity?

And there would be a benefit to the cities, which have the universities students would want to attend. The postsecondary education sector generates considerable economic activity: jobs for teachers, administrators, and service people; sales opportunities for suppliers of food, books, clothing, and housing; more passengers for transit systems and taxis; more shoppers, diners, movie-goers, and patients.

Such a program should ensure that the participating universities go to great lengths to be welcoming to this new cadre of students from around the world—not a quality that Canadian universities can boast about now. To qualify, they should show they have great bridging programs for language and culture, sympathetic and attentive faculty advisors, health and psychology professionals able to intervene appropriately, and student bodies that are enthusiastic and organized to welcome the newcomers. What a wonderful journey it would be for our great universities to prepare themselves to be truly international, a united mission by a whole campus community, including alumni and financial supporters.

The federal government could do much to enhance the cultural life of cities by using the tax system to encourage developers to incorporate cultural space into new developments, or in major renovations of existing buildings. Vancouver offers a good example of what can be done, although the cultural amenities there have resulted from the city planning department's density-trading practices. If a developer agrees to incorporate a cultural element—say, a gallery or theatre—in the building, and puts aside an endowment that can be applied against operating funds, then the city planning department will allow them to build some additional floors that will yield the additional revenue necessary to offset the cultural obligations. Using the tax system, the federal government could do the same thing. Provided that the new amenity was compatible with the intentions of the city, the federal government could offer a tax credit that would make the costs associated either partly or wholly deductible from the income of the project. This could be applied in favour of arts and cultural groups, but also for other charities in aid of providing office space, workshop facilities, and meeting rooms. Including the deposit of a significant sum of money as an endowment, or a fund to be drawn down gradually, can augment the stability of the space itself by providing money to mitigate operating costs.

An example of what might be done is the Contemporary Art Gallery in Vancouver. Established in the late 1970s, the CAG was housed in an old single room occupancy hotel in a gritty part of downtown. As a result of a City of Vancouver "bonus" arrangement with the developer, Bosa Ventures Incorporated, the gallery now has a new 5,600-square-foot home at the base of a new development at 555 Nelson Street. It is a handsome modern gallery with two exhibition spaces and necessary library and curatorial space. As a result of the bonus arrangement, Bosa was permitted to add four floors to one of its towers, and three to the other. And the CAG was able to move into an appealing new home that was not only more attractive to gallery goers, but that gave it a much stronger platform from which to operate its fundraising activities.

Another way that the federal government could stimulate the cultural life of cities is by dedicating some of the taxes collected there to supporting culture. For example, by sharing a part of the airplane ticket surcharge paid by passengers departing the city airport, they could create a fund that the city could distribute to libraries, symphony halls, and sports arenas. After all, these cultural activities are significant elements underpinning local tourism, for which the airports are major gateways. Or the federal government could leave behind some of the airport landing fees they charge. There's plenty of room, particularly in the big cities. Toronto's Pearson Airport, for example, has 33 percent of the landings in Canada, but contributes 63 percent of the landing fees. And the other big airports probably pay disproportionately beyond what their traffic would warrant. The idea of earmarking tax revenue for something related to the tax is an idea much beloved of tax experts, but not necessarily of tax collectors, who love to have full freedom to spend the funds as they wish.

Immigrants: Attaching Funding to Individuals

Immigrant settlement is a critical national activity that occurs locally. The federal government has made grants to provinces to support settlement work, to house, educate, acclimatize, and employ newcomers. But the regional disparities that have developed over the years have been alarming. In 2002, Quebec was getting $3,808 per immigrant, while Ontario was getting $819—a disparity that was only eliminated after outraged reactions from the Ontario government and the array of agencies serving immigrants in the Toronto region. (Quebec was receiving 15.4 percent of immigrants, compared with 57.4 percent in Ontario.) And the provinces were often diverting the money from direct support of settlement to other needs. What is worse, when the immigrant moved from Montreal to Toronto, for example, the payment attributed to her stayed in Quebec and didn't follow her to Toronto. The federal government could reconsider these transfers as direct payments to people, and have them follow the person around no matter where they live. They could apply standards as to what the payments would cover so that they were not spent on things that government did not consider to be critical elements of settlement. They could be refundable tax credits, requiring receipts or documentation from city-operated programs, or other certified program operators. Such an approach would create some equity in the treatment of immigrants, no matter where they chose to settle. Of course, different cities have different costs, so there could be some indexing of the payments based on comparative costs between cities.

There are also ways that the federal government could empower cities that don't necessarily involve money. They could create a seat at the table for cities whenever matters in which the city has expertise and interest are being considered. Immigrant settlement is one obvious such area. Cities have the longest and deepest experience in settling immigrants, and to construct policy and programs without them at the table makes little sense. Similarly, cities have a huge interest and significant experience in issues related to the environment. Waste management, sewage, provision of clean water, management of storm waters and rain water, vehicular emissions, transit provision, parks, and tree canopies are all central to the management of the city, and all have immense influence over environmental outcomes. To construct a national environmental policy and related programs without a close consultation with the major urban regions is folly.

No Free Lunch

While measures taken through the tax system or by direct payments to people are ways for the federal government to affect what happens in cities without stepping on the provinces' toes, they are not without problems. The first one is that they cost money. There is no free money, no free ride, no free lunch. A tax credit or benefit is not free: the federal government gives up tax revenues. In terms of the impact on the federal treasury, there is no difference between a tax measure and a gift or grant. What a credit or benefit would allow the federal government to do is target financial support without dealing directly with the city government, and without having to funnel the money through the provincial government. Ottawa doesn't want to do the former because the provinces would complain that their territory is being infringed upon. The federal government doesn't want to do the latter for fear the provinces will divert the money to something else.

The other problem in proposing such approaches is that the federal government has to actually want to help the cities. In recent decades in Canada, it is far from clear that this is the case. Diffidence has ruled the day. Ottawa seems unconcerned that it is standing alone as the only national government in the developed world that washes its hands of the key needs of its major cities, avoiding housing and transportation programs and stinting on much else. One can propose all the mechanisms and channels in the world for them to come to the assistance of the cities, but if they don't want to do it in the first place, not much will happen. As they say in rural Canada, you can lead a horse to water but you can't make him drink. The federal government seems to be guided by such homespun truths.

This is frustrating for the cities, and for their advocates who think we need to seek new strategies more actively. If we cannot identify and put into play such simple and actionable approaches that don't defy any constitutional taboos or violate sensibilities, is there any hope for change?

And if there is no hope for change on those terms, perhaps change has to come about more dramatically, with a few bumps and twists. And if that doesn't work, maybe we need to rethink the country from the ground up. Maybe federal torpor, and the chains of the Constitution, will finally move us to rise up.

The Way Forward: Some Incremental Program Steps

Transit

- Make transit passes tax-deductible, with personal deductions for individuals and the ability for businesses to categorize costs as business expenses.
- Provide guarantees for sinking funds and tax increment financing to fund transit capital projects.

Housing

- Permit the rollover of capital gains into new low-income housing projects, with the capital gains tax paid only on the accumulated gain after the investor has ceased low-income housing investment.

- Permit accelerated depreciation of reinvestment in new low-income projects.
- Rebate GST on low-income projects.
- Create a refundable tax credit for rental or mortgage payments, aimed at low-income people.

Education
- Create the equivalent of the Millennium Scholarship Fund for students from developing countries to study at Canadian universities and colleges.

Culture
- Create a tax credit for property developers who incorporate cultural space into new developments.
- Earmark tax surcharges on things like airplane tickets to support local cultural or recreation facilities.

Immigrant Settlement
- Attach funding to individual immigrants, perhaps as a refundable tax credit, that they can take with them wherever they move in the country, using it to acquire services from qualified suppliers.
- Create a "seat at the table" for the big-city regions in the design of immigration policy and programs.

9

GLORIOUS AND FREE
Bigger Steps for a Brighter Future

Baby steps are for babies. Our modern city regions have long since outgrown the adequacy of small, incremental steps towards the future, and their relative decline in recent decades is an indictment of such slow and hard-won progress. That is not to say that the incremental steps should be abandoned or ignored, but they will be inadequate by themselves. Most of the baby steps outlined in the previous chapter should probably be taken, and many more with them, because they offer practical and attainable changes that will benefit people and the country. But each one is hard to come by, requiring years and sometimes decades of proposals and appeals, of pushing and persuading over and over again. Years of effort may be rewarded with a half-measure or less, and constant pressure afterwards may eke out an enhancement now and again. It is a long, hard road to the future.

And that long, hard road lies next to a superhighway on which everything is whizzing by at breakneck speed, the pace at which the world is operating. It is the pace of technological change, and the pace at which people are moving ahead with their lives. Governments, more than ever, are playing catch-up, unable to keep pace with where people are taking society. In commerce, education, science, medicine, culture, and communication, the world is racing ahead and governments are looking increasingly dazed and laggardly. Baby steps won't help when what is required is at least a spirited trot, if not a sprint.

Baby steps have not only been proven inadequate, but cities have become so used to them that they don't know how to move more boldly. It is common to hear politicians at the federal and provincial levels decry municipal politicians for their infantile ways, their inability to act with maturity and cohesion. So they treat municipalities like babies; and, as a result, many of them act like babies and slip further behind.

Incremental steps must give way to giant steps. And giant steps must bundle together small measures into larger instruments of change. A transfer of powers from the federal and provincial governments to the large-city regions is the most appropriate giant step to take. Rather than telling cities how to behave one issue at a time, governments should give the cities broad authority and responsibility to control their own destinies. This seems counterintuitive to many who think the cities aren't up to the job. But they are apt to be very pleasantly surprised at how capable the cities are at meeting the challenge.

After all, cities are highly competent at many things. They deliver hard infrastructure like roads, bridges, transit systems, water, and sewage very well. They provide human services very well. They run school systems, public health programs, and cultural programs very well. There is little to suggest that they would not handle other things well. There may be learning curves for new services, but these exist for all levels of government. One only has to read reports from various government's auditors general to understand that there is an ever-present learning curve, and in some cases plain inadequacy at the federal and provincial levels.

So, in terms of powers, governance, and finance, it is time to move boldly and establish a more effective platform from which Canada can move into the future. And what, short of reinventing the country, does that platform look like?

Turn Vancouver, Toronto, and Montreal into City-Provinces

In essence, it involves giving the three big-city regions the powers of a province. And giving the next tier of cities a strong set of powers that may fall just short of that. Exactly which cities, and which powers, will depend to a good extent on the regional context within which the cities sit. For example, in Alberta, Edmonton and Calgary account for over two-thirds of the population of the province, although they only contain about half of the ridings in the legislature, and should theoretically be able to tilt government policy to be attentive to the urban needs of those two places. But Greater Vancouver represents about half of the BC population, and only a third of the seats, and might use some more independent powers to have more command over its future. As would Toronto in Ontario and Montreal in Quebec.

The Greater Toronto Area (GTA) has a population of about 5.6 million, and if one takes into account the effective economic area known as the Greater Golden Horseshoe (GGH) around the western end of Lake Ontario and extending to Kitchener-Waterloo, the figure rises to about 8.5 million, about 25 percent of Canada's population. Prince Edward Island, with all the powers of a province, has a population of less than 150,000. Each of the Maritime provinces, and each of the Prairie provinces, has fewer people than the GTA. All of them combined have a smaller population than the GGH, yet they can handle the powers of a province. Vancouver, the smallest of the large urban regions, has more people than six of the ten provinces, as does Montreal.

It is not, of course, just a question of population. It is more precisely a matter of governments being able to serve most directly the needs and interests of their citizens. Given most governments' unwillingness to provide differentiated solutions across their domains, the more varied and disparate those needs and interests are, the more likely it is that citizens will be asked to don ill-fitting "one-size-fits-all" garments. An effort to construct political jurisdictions with some strong coherence of needs and interests can result in more effective government. In the Canadian context there are dramatic ways to try this, but recent experience with Constitutional reform has made us shy away from that. What is needed is a lower-impact way of getting there, but something considerably more effective than the incremental, baby-step approach.

The best solution is to create three city regions with the powers and status of provinces. They would be the urban regions around Toronto, Montreal, and Vancouver. A number of things separate these three regions from the next tier of cities.

1. They are bigger. Vancouver is the smallest, with a metropolitan region of about 2.2 million people. Montreal has 3.7 million and Toronto 5.6 million. Taking into account the economic reach of those cities, the regions grow even larger. (Ontario provincial government officials used to consider the Toronto ambit to include places where one could get same-day home delivery of the *Toronto Star*.)

2. They have complex economies, not reliant on one or two industries or employers. Calgary is still heavily reliant on the oil industry to underpin its economy, although there has been some diversification in recent years. Such cities as Edmonton, Winnipeg, Quebec City, Halifax, and Ottawa are heavily reliant on govern-

ment offices and institutions. Urban regions with complex economies have more resilience. If one industry or a major corporation goes away, the impact is fairly small. The complexity itself feeds the economy, providing a ready resource of seasoned executives and workers who can move from company to company, industry to industry. These three regions also have solid infrastructures of other institutions of education, health care, social services, and arts and culture that can offer a range of opportunities for building human and social capital.

3. These regions are an agglomeration of towns and cities that have grown together. Early settlements in Vancouver began around New Westminster, now a component city of Greater Vancouver somewhat southeast of where downtown has grown, and the city has spread eastward up the Fraser River valley and south across the Fraser Delta. Montreal still has strong local identities, as evidenced by the amalgamation and deamalgamation that occurred recently. The former mayor of the Town of Mount Royal still commands media attention as he articulates the needs and issues of his community. In Toronto, a decade after the 1997 amalgamation, people still identify not only with the former cities of Etobicoke, York, or Scarborough, but with towns and villages from half a century before, like Swansea and Mount Dennis, that are now part of Toronto. Therefore, there are quite complicated political arrangements across the region that might benefit from a new local political structure able to focus on local issues.

4. They are where immigrants settle, at scale. Thus they have a critical mass of newcomers, which presents unique challenges for the delivery of such public services as health care, education, housing, and settlement. Of course, other cities get some immigrants—notably, places like Ottawa and Hamilton—but at current rates it

is the big three city regions that have received, and will receive, the bulk of them. And they would benefit from a capacity to respond quickly, based on their experience.

Other countries have city regions with a different status from most of the cities in the country. In Germany, there are three city regions that have the status of provinces, or *landers*: Berlin, Bremen, and Hamburg. They have the same powers and responsibilities as the other German states. Their relationship with the federal state is not perfect, and they have arguments about taxation tools, boundaries, and authority. In fact, several of the *landers* have significantly different rights and responsibilities; studying them is somewhat like eating an artichoke, in that there is more on the plate when you finish than when you started.

In Austria, Vienna is a state equal to the other eight that make up the country, enjoying the same powers and responsibilities. In France, Paris is a "department," and the urban region is one of the "regions" of France. As both a department and a region, Paris enjoys considerable authority. A look across the rest of Europe sees urban regions singled out for special status: Moscow and St. Petersburg in Russia; Ceuta and Melilla, Spain's north African outposts; Vatican City in the middle of Rome; Monaco in southern France. And looking farther abroad, Singapore was originally part of Malaysia before being granted independence in 1965. Buenos Aires became an "autonomous region" in Argentina in 1996, with direct representation in the national legislature. Across the world, there are city regions that participate in national life on the same basis as other political regions in the country.

If one can accept the idea of city-regions acting like provinces within the Canadian context, it would be important to know what powers they would have. If they are generally to be "the powers of a province," what precisely might these be? A place to start would be with the two big areas of provincial activity, health care and education.

Urban Health Care Needs Are Different from Those Outside Cities

That cities have particular health care needs arises in part out of their status as the places where immigrants settle. Immigrants have different needs from the health care system in terms of both pathology and care protocols. That is, what they might have to be treated for, and the manner of care, can both be different. Any number of studies, as well as the accumulated experience of city-based doctors and public health officials, tell the same story. People coming to Canada, the US, or European countries from the developing world generally come from a less sophisticated health care environment. Sometimes the system in their home country has been more oriented to explaining disease, so as to help the community and family deal with it, than to treating it. Western medicine, some argue, is more oriented to identifying and treating a problem and less concerned with its community context. Sometimes the country of origin is under stress, and not able to afford or distribute successfully the necessary testing requirements or medicines.

The Centers for Disease Control and Prevention in Atlanta reports that immigrants to the US have a higher incidence than the domestic population of tuberculosis, hepatitis B, stool parasites, and leprosy, and are much more likely to have either no or lapsed immunizations. Tuberculosis, a disease thought to be eradicated in the West (although it seems to be making a comeback, as predicted by people like Ivan Illich years ago), is prevalent in the developing world. Some estimates say two billion people are infected, with less than 5 percent of those becoming active. Immigrants become active cases at a rate five times that of people born in the US. Hepatitis C and HIV are also more common among immigrants, and there is some indication that the drugs prescribed may vary in effectiveness depending on the country of origin and accompanying diseases. Parasites are also more various and complicated. They can survive for years in a person, and can often require multiple tests to detect.

Infectious-disease experts detect patterns of germ development in various places around the world, and dream of early-detection systems in those hotspots in order to prepare destination cities for the arrival of the next SARS. But there is no assurance that those destination cities would be adept at dealing with the information, particularly if they were part of a provincial health system that "averaged down" treatment in a way that prevented quick and appropriate response to new diseases.

New treatments are one thing, but new protocols of care are another. Culturally diverse populations, which we have in Vancouver, Montreal, and Toronto, bring with them a variety of approaches to care. One dimension of this is found in the diagnostic process. In some cultures, having tuberculosis or HIV is not something that is readily admitted, and so the questions or instructions that might work in Canada might not work with a particular newcomer. Often, the language barrier disrupts detection as the translator might not get the words right—for instance, if they opt for a literal translation that doesn't mean anything in translation. Sometimes the patient doesn't want to be candid in front of a translator. The translator or doctor might have a bias, or there could be questions of status, a different perception of the relative roles of patients and doctors, and issues of power and politics that might influence the ways people from different cultures see things. These are often present in any doctor-patient discussion, but can be amplified by the presence of an intermediary. And that is just during the diagnostic phase.

When it comes to treatment, cultural differences can have a huge impact, again often exacerbated by language barriers. How much of a body can be viewed? Can a male doctor look at a woman patient, or a female doctor at a male patient? What kind of poking and probing can be done, and where? Who else might, or must, be present during examination and treatment? Once patient and family get away from the doctor, is the medical advice still dominant, or does father—or another local authority figure—prevail in the name of honour, austerity, or tradition?

This isn't a comment on a good approach versus a bad one. It is merely an observation about different ways of doing things. In fact, the health care system has been dealing with such differences for years. Jehovah's Witnesses refuse blood transfusions and other forms of medical intervention. Doctors and nurses don't like it, but they have dealt with it. But with increased migration, and rapidly growing and changing source countries, these professionals have to adapt even more quickly. Good health care systems are good at managing these changes, and have put in place comprehensive training and mediation capabilities to increase the chance of successful patient care. Canadian big-city hospitals are pretty good in this regard, but they would benefit from the ability to focus more resources in building this capacity.

City Schools Teach Different Things

Schools are similar. I walked through the yard of my old school in Vancouver a few years ago, while poking around the old neighbourhood. That night at dinner with some old classmates I made a comment heard all the time in Vancouver, Toronto, and other immigrant-receiving cities: that the racial makeup of the kids was dramatically different from when I went there. Of course, I was walking through the schoolyard about five decades later. There are schools in Toronto where that change happens every decade. These are the schools where the halls are filled with the sound of languages other than English and French, a glorious cacophony of tongues all animated by the universal song of children talking.

As a school takes on a new identity through successive waves of new faces, it needs to equip itself—much as a hospital does—with people who can translate and who can counsel the students on how to do the work well—and the parents on how they can help. They need to have some capacity to mediate conflict, in case the new population is one of those at risk of bringing old world conflicts to their new world. Schools with Sri Lankans might include both Tamils and Sinhalese; those with Rwandans might include Tutsis and Hutus. They are not necessarily going to have conflicts, but making sure that schools had a good mediation capacity, either resident or quickly available, would be wise.

The particular complexities in urban schools are not just related to newcomers. The fact of families with two working parents, or single-parent families, also present issues of what kids do after school, with whom and where. School systems need to be able to respond quickly to changing community conditions, in the interest of the children and their ability to learn. They need to be able to defend the children against gangs, another urban phenomenon, and the myriad other ways for kids to become lost. The less school systems have to fight against a central authority that is trying to design and apply single solutions across a whole range of communities, the more they can be particular and focused in their response to the observed and expressed needs of the children, and the better served those kids— and their parents, and the whole community—will be.

One example was the attempt to ensure the inclusion of anti-racism content in the curricula of Ontario schools, a project that had been under development over a number of years—and under governments representing various ruling parties—by the ministry of education. It was a response to the growing diversity in the schools, particularly in the cities. Then, in response to the Yonge Street riot in May of 1992, the Rae government directed all of its ministries to develop bold anti-racism activities that included a government-wide anti-racism secretariat. In education, an assistant deputy minister was appointed with responsibility for "anti-racism, access, and equity." Plans were underway to ensure that the entire leadership of Ontario's education system would undergo anti-racism training, and a strategy to ensure a more diverse teaching force was fully developed. But in 1995, the government of Mike Harris abruptly cancelled these initiatives. A Harris aide advised the minister and deputy minister to "get rid of it." And over time, all of the other government-wide initiatives were halted as well.

It was clear that Harris's electoral support had not come from the city, and there was little perceived need for anti-racism training in suburban and rural ridings. Thus, Harris's cabinet concluded it could be slashed as another small-l liberal frill. Ten years later, in the summer of 2005, there was a spate of gun violence, which caught people like Mike Harris off guard. Where did that come from? When educators and journalists drew a line back to the earlier decision to cut the anti-racism content from the schools, the argument was disparaged as too simplistic. But the fact is that few urban-based educators thought the programming should have been cut, and if curriculum had been in the hands of city-based educators, it and much else related to cultural diversity would have been retained.

Local control over the curriculum flies in the face of such ideas as "province-wide" testing and uniform standards. There is a notion of equity that says the child in Barry's Bay, the beautiful community in eastern Ontario, should be learning exactly the same thing as a child in the Malvern neighbourhood in Toronto, or a kid in Attawapiskat on the coast of James Bay or in the Glebe in Ottawa. This notion runs counter to the particularity with which we all live our lives. Certainly we can all share a need to add, parse, write, and dissect. But there is considerably less need for me to be able to read ice conditions than a man in Attawapiskat, to recognize soil composition than a potato farmer in Lisle, or know spruce budworm on sight than a forester in Elliot Lake. Local control of school systems can include the particularities of local conditions.

The creation of province-like entities in Vancouver, Montreal, and Toronto would enable the school systems to construct their budgets to reflect local choices and priorities, such as cultural sensitivity, after-school programs for "latch-key kids," arts, or sports (including sports such as cricket that are gaining in popularity).

Immigration Is Urban

Immigrant settlement would be a principal beneficiary of new city-provinces. As has been noted earlier, the big-city regions have the longest and deepest experience in settlement. Allowing them to design policy and programs, and have the revenue tools to pay for them, would mean that adequate housing could be made available for the annual waves of newcomers. Cities could plan and develop a comprehensive stock of housing that could serve not only the new-comer community, but could provide a progressive range of accom-modations that could move people from "starter" to family homes, and from rental to ownership. For cities, the availability of housing is not a sideline that can be addressed with sporadic small gestures; it is a core necessity. Similarly, the provision of bridging and adjustment programs for newcomers to facilitate their access to the labour market, the education system, the health care system, and government services is of high importance to accelerate their becoming full contributing members of society. Immigrants have been immense assets to Canada, as almost every mayor in the country will attest. Getting them fully up to speed, shoulder to shoulder with those who came before, is a critical national objective, but one that is recognized most acutely in the cities. City-provinces would reflect that priority through budgetary and programming commitments far beyond what now occurs.

Environment Policy Is Most Critical in Cities

Environment is another critical area for city regions, one that is clearly perceived with less urgency at the provincial and particularly the federal level. At the national level, recent governments have been rhetorically in flight, but with their feet stuck in the mud. Whatever paltry progress was being made by the Chrétien and Martin governments has been reeled in by the Harper government and its unlikely environment minister, John Baird. Provincial governments, which actually contain the big cities where pollution gets concentrated, have been a little better, but still slow. And it is often their land-use policies, in their laxness and laissez-faire tendencies, that have encouraged the oozing sprawl that is choking the urban regions in traffic jams and carbon monoxide haze. Transit is one way to reduce congestion and pollution, but the key is better land-use planning. We are just beginning to wake up to the critical importance of land-use decisions that have enormous environmental outcomes, which we've known about for some time, but also critical social outcomes. Isolating people in low-density subdivisions with cul-de-sac roads and few local social or commercial outlets, making them completely dependent on cars to get in and out, can affect their physical and mental health, their employment opportunities, their education options, and their capacity to connect socially—a critical factor in well-being and in participation in civic life. This last matter is perhaps the one with the sharpest bite, as we have watched voter participation rates drop as we've seen sprawl increase, and we've seen poll after poll document the rising disassociation of citizens from the vital machinery of our democracy. City regions need the capacity to intervene in this decline, to make democracy vital again, and local control over land use decisions and patterns of growth is absolutely crucial.

Cities Need Tough Gun Laws

Perhaps no issue is more indicative of the need for new city-provinces than gun control. Canada has hard-won gun control laws and a gun registry system, despite much political controversy and inexcusable cost overruns by slack public officials. In rural Canada, they think these measures represent an infringement on some supposed rights they have and an example of government gone out of control. In the cities, they wish the laws were tougher; indeed, many city-dwellers wonder why anybody needs a gun for anything. Mayors and police chiefs in the big cities would like to take away the guns and enact harsh laws that would penalize the scofflaws. In the middle are moderate views that question the need for automatic weapons or handguns, while conceding that hunters would like to have rifles and shotguns available to take into the bush with them. And pretty well everyone recognizes the ongoing needs of traditional hunters to provide their livelihood, particularly in the sparsely populated north. A city-province could, and should, pass strong laws, as long as they would "meet or beat" the federal law. And they could do so without having to worry about getting on the wrong side of someone living near Fort St. John, Hornepayne, or Chibougamau, places whose laws could be more appropriate to the conditions in which the people live.

Housing and transit have both been discussed here, and in both cases cities need to be able to act consistently—to ensure that supply doesn't fall behind demand in a way that would create insurmountable backlogs—and quickly, to respond to sudden upticks in demand. In both of these capital-intensive areas, cities need control of destiny in order to provide the long-range predictability on which financing can be arranged. And they need to have confidence that things won't be abruptly changed by another level of government, disabling the finance, and destroying the coordination between housing and transportation that is so critical to efficiency.

The advantage of a city-province would be that local conditions would more directly affect local law and regulation. There would be fewer requirements to "average down" measures to meet needs, to mitigate effective responses because of the needs and interests of people who live far away and differently. There is, some argue, value in negotiating compromises between conflicting needs and interests, in that it produces durable solutions and a resilient society that knows how to settle differences. But in a competitive world, where economic, social, and cultural assets are tremendously mobile, city regions need to be able to react quickly to keep pace with competitors and to capitalize on opportunity.

Shall Canada Continue to Fail Its Cities Conventionally, or Risk Succeeding Unconventionally?

Of course, there is a long, hard road to the creation of city-provinces. Anyone who has witnessed the attempts at constitutional reorganization in Canada knows about the many milestones and bumps along the way. John Maynard Keynes noted that for one's reputation it was often better to fail conventionally than succeed unconventionally. He applied this to matters of finance and investment, but it could equally be applied to Canada's behaviour in reconsidering our political arrangements. We know that the current setup has all sorts of problems, but we'd rather keep doing what we've always done, even if it means getting what we always got. So we are quick to point out the problems of change, and we let them obscure the advantages.

The quickest way to cast doubt on a proposed change like creating city-provinces is to raise the issue of boundaries. Who is in, and who is out? If Vancouver is to become a city-province, is Richmond in, or out? What about Langley, or White Rock, or Whistler? Or in the case of Montreal, what about communities along the south shore? And how far along the south shore? And who decides who is in and who is out? Is it the province from which the city-province is to be carved? A joint commission of the city and province?

And which city? If it is to be a city-province negotiation in Ontario, for example, are all the potentially included cities at the negotiation table? If they are, do they get weighted votes? The town of Caledon could be included, but the city of Mississauga has over ten times as many residents, and the city of Toronto has forty times as many. It could be a complicated negotiation—perhaps too complicated. There could be gridlock and defeat.

The issue of boundaries can create unnecessary divisions before the substance of terms and conditions are even drafted, let alone tabled. People get very wedded to the turf they occupy, and fear usurpation. Professor Andrew Sancton of the University of Western Ontario, a leading authority on municipal amalgamations, has recently turned his attention to the inherent complexity of boundaries and has concluded that they form such a massive barrier to change that change-makers should seek a less difficult way to deal with the pressing issues cities face. Changing city boundaries requires an authority from outside the area in question to impose the change—an authority like a province—so why not leave things as they are, with the province acting as the effective ultimate authority over cities?

And the formal methodology the country has adopted for constitutional change sets hard criteria. Seven of the ten provincial legislatures, representing 50 percent of the population, need to approve. This is a hard measure to achieve, and the issue of adding new provinces that were once cities would be seen by many of the smaller provinces as an attempt to outnumber them. In a country so attentive to regional and minority interests, formal constitutional reform is unlikely.

However, a province could decide to create a new entity within its own boundaries, one that would have all the powers of a province, without appealing to the rest of the country for approval. So, if the province of British Columbia decided that Vancouver should be like a province, it could create such an entity and empower it appropriately. For everything that entailed relations with the province, there would be no problems. For relations with the national government, should there be resistance from the federal government or other parts of the country, the province could act as a surrogate for the new city-province. It could participate in the national system of transfer payments on the new entity's behalf. It could create effective parallel processes that would precisely mimic independent status, until such time as the federation realized that the change was at worst benign.

In fact, provinces could create internally several echelons of empowered cities. A truly brave province could express the view that cities can be differentiated by size and complexity, as Premier Dalton McGuinty did in Ontario. So, to use the BC example, Vancouver could be established as a fully autonomous city-region with all the powers of a province. And Victoria might be designated an A-class city, with many of the powers of a province, but plugging into the overall provincial apparatus in key ways. This would not be all that difficult a change for the three provinces in question, for they all have, to some extent, individual relations with the cities under their purview. And in the cases of the fully autonomous city regions, they would actually be ceasing to do a number of things, instead focusing energy and attention on managing a new set of tiered arrangements.

There are various ways to achieve the creation of a city-province. The easiest, but perhaps least desirable, is for the province to act unilaterally and declare the creation of an autonomous city-region, set the boundaries, and create the legal and political framework. This has happened before: between 1968 and 1974, the Ontario government created regional governments; again in 1996, when the province amalgamated the constituent cities of Metropolitan Toronto into the new City of Toronto. The province has the power to do such things, and the cities cannot resist. They can object, as they have always done at such high-handedness, and the objection can taint the political environment to such an extent that decades later there are still lingering resentments, and periodic political roadblocks that get erected. Mississauga mayor Hazel McCallion still bridles at the shared jurisdiction with the Regional Municipality of Peel under its chair, Emil Kolb. The Toronto amalgamation was handled abruptly and in the face of heated opposition from city residents and politicians; a decade later neither the administrative arrangements nor the politics had been sorted out. The provincial architects of the amalgamation thought the administration would work itself out within one three-year term of office, and the politics in two terms. They weren't even close.

So, acting via provincial dictate may seem simpler at the outset, but is likely to be more complicated in the long run. The basic problem is that creating a new political entity is complicated. Untangling old arrangements and establishing durable new ones is complex and multi-dimensional, even when it seems simple. Something as basic seeming as the interoperability of ambulance systems—allowing ambulance drivers to cross city limits to deliver patients to a hospital—has to be pushed through a thicket of issues. Are the workers in each jurisdiction equally paid, and unionized, and bonded? Are insurance liabilities covered once an ambulance crosses the boundary? Are the procedures and protocols for handling patients in sync? How does the money work? Will the ambulance service get paid, and by whom? And those are just the practical questions. What about the politics of sending a person from one jurisdiction to another, particularly if something goes wrong and it hits the newspapers or television newscast? How does the accountability work?

None of these are unanswerable questions, but some of them might not be anticipated. A process of creating city-provinces that takes time to consider the specifics of new arrangements, rather than leaving them to be worked out later, can identify points of difficulty or conflict and allow time for them to be worked out.

There are a couple of ways this might be done. A commission might be struck to consider and recommend the creation of the new city-province. Who sits on such a commission is always a critical question. Often it is "interested" people—perhaps, in this case, local mayors and councillors—and such discussions often dissolve into turf wars and rehashing of old resentments. Sometimes it is a random group of citizens, a "citizen's assembly," many of whom have steep learning curves to acquire a productive relationship to the subject matter. And sometimes it is a panel of eminent people, with the idea that their eminence will make it harder for the government of the day to ignore what they come up with.

It might be useful to look at what has worked in Canada in recent years in dealing with difficult and complex issues. The surprising answer, at least for most Canadians, would be the Canadian Senate. Much maligned—in fact, with few defenders—the Senate of Canada has an exemplary record when it comes to considering tough national questions. The press has focused on the periodic confrontations between the government and Senate over things like free trade, the implementation of the Goods and Services Tax, and the clarity bill, or on the occasional senator found living in retirement in a Mexican villa. But the Senate has an excellent record in reviewing and amending legislation emanating from the House of Commons, and in investigating issues. In recent decades, the Senate has produced sound analysis and recommendations on banking and financial services, euthanasia and assisted suicide, veterans' affairs, fisheries, foreign affairs, and health care. While the press has been busy looking for what parliamentary expert C.E.S. Franks calls "blood on the floor" and partisan conflict, the Senate has worked through its committees in a largely nonpartisan way. Because members of the Senate have a duty to Canada, a significantly longer tenure than members of the House of Commons (who serve on average for little more than four years), a more varied and diverse life experience than MPs, and no electoral pressure, they can devote themselves to the task of investigating and considering complex issues.

If the Senate itself proves not to be the place to consider the creation of city-provinces, the model of a Royal commission of thoughtful, experienced people with the time and resources to consider each new polity makes sense. Such commissions could be struck in BC, Ontario, and Quebec to consider the particularity of each situation and recommend appropriately. These commissions would take a broad range of public inputs, some solicited or commissioned, so that interests and aspirations could be included. Ultimately, the commissions would produce recommendations describing the new regions in terms of powers, finances, and governance structure. Then the thorny question of boundaries would have to be addressed—who is in, who is out?

There is a relatively simple way to deal with this, and it is by an opting-in process. When the issue of Quebec separation was alive in the 1980s and '90s, many areas of the province were not keen on separating, and the question of partition arose. If Quebec was divisible from Canada, went the argument, so might parts of the province be from the whole, and they could stay with Canada. While this was not an argument that held much sway, it at least introduced the possibility that some areas might opt in while others opted out. So it might be with a new city-province arrangement. To take Toronto as an example, a commission might recommend that the current City of Toronto be created with the powers of a province, and it would spell out the powers, financial arrangements, and governance structure. Then there would be a process whereby the neighbouring cities would be able to put up their hands and say, "We want in." The objective would be to have as much of a contiguous region as possible included, so the commission would want to make the powers, finances, and governance as attractive as possible. Thus, when the neighbouring cities looked at the new arrangements, they would have to present real and substantive choices between aligning with the new state or remaining under the ambit of the province. And because the new state would express much in the way of local particularity, it would likely ally locally.

A third way is to act incrementally. Across each of the three urban regions in question, there are already a number of functional bodies working to coordinate services across regions. Transportation is a key one. Vancouver has TransLink; the Toronto region has the new Metrolinx (formerly the Greater Toronto Transportation Authority) trying to coordinate seventeen local transit systems under the chairmanship of former mayor Rob McIsaac of Burlington. Montreal has the Agence métropolitaine de transport. And a look at any municipal function will find both more and less successful coordination efforts in such areas as waste management, water and sewage, social services, settlement services, and public health. Many of these operate on an ad hoc basis, without any vision that they contribute to a larger whole. They usually operate over varying geography, including different participating cities and towns—some solely on a government-to-government basis, while others include nongovernment organizations and other institutions. In fact, these informal arrangements are part of the magic fabric that makes cities work so well. Jane Jacobs always argued that you could rely to a considerable extent on people figuring out how to work together, how to cobble together solutions that were effective and durable. She preferred to let these solutions bubble up from experience and practice rather than imposing a template from outside or above.

These functional cooperative practices can be increased and knit together. Creating incentives around revenue generation and effective outcomes can increase the range of activities, and the regional fabric can become denser and richer. And because they are rooted in the most practical requirements of the region, they are more immune to the play of politics, turf protection, and other interference.

Of course, incrementalism can last forever, and move at such a glacial pace that things will look roughly the same a century from now. Incremental change, to be effective, must outpace the normal pace of change. So it would make sense to set some time frames around the creation of such cross-regional bodies, and some notional objectives around the creation of larger regional governance and autonomy measures. A decade seems reasonable.

So, by 2020, we could see a Canada with thirteen provinces, effectively, including the newcomers of Vancouver, Toronto, and Montreal.

Each might have a different form of government. Some might be a federation of member cities, a metropolitan form of two-tier government. Some might have a unitary government. Some might have virtual autonomous status; some might use their provincial government apparatus to mimic autonomy. All would have access to a broad range of revenue tools, such as the right to levy a broad range of taxes including income and sales taxes, all could issue debt and engage in modern financing instruments the way real governments can. All would have the authority to alter their own form of government, as long as it complied with Canadian law. And all would be components of the Canadian federation, electing members to Parliament in Ottawa, as they do now.

These are bold steps, which would require bold premiers in BC, Ontario, and Quebec. It would also require boldness on the part of other politicians in Canada, who would have to be willing to succeed unconventionally, or at least let others try to succeed. It would be a true test of Canada's willingness to compete in the modern world, and a test of its leaders.

Bold Steps

- Creation of sub-provinces of Vancouver, Toronto, and Montreal by the provinces of British Columbia, Ontario, and Quebec respectively.
- Extension of powers of provinces to Vancouver, Toronto, and Montreal, including independent control over health and education systems and access to the full range of revenue instruments (taxes and debt) that provinces have.
- Creation of a set of more autonomous tolls in each province to give cities larger than 500,000 more control of their destinies, yet less than full provincial powers.

10

THE TRUE NORTH
A New Canada for the Twenty-First Century

If Canada's Fathers of Confederation were meeting now, at the outset of the twenty-first century, they would create a very different country. Of course, their numbers would include Mothers of Confederation as well, but that would not be the major difference. They would look at the realities of present-day Canada and make choices that would speak to the challenges of the time, as Sir John A. Macdonald and his colleagues did 140 years ago. Then, the task was to cobble together the former British and French colonial units that had not become part of the United States of America, and they did it with political energy, canny deal-making, and a slew of visions that galvanized around the remarkable strength of Macdonald. Essentially, they made the country they could at the time. There were existing forces of history, geography, politics, and human nature that resulted in the federation that thrives to this day.

A group of twenty-first-century architects of Confederation would encounter similar realities of history and politics that would circumscribe the possibilities. Interestingly, many of those realities are similar to those in 1867. The strong French identity of Quebec continues, with its distinctive language and culture. The sense of identity of each of the provinces remains—perhaps not as strongly as in Quebec, but still there. The regionalism of the country remains, perhaps exacerbated over the decades by politicians looking for points of purchase, or discord. And the practice of federalism over our history, the deal-making that has gone on between the nation and the provinces, has made everything negotiable. Therefore, any redrafting of the country would never be a simple matter, but a subject of protracted debate and bargaining.

Of course, wisdom would caution against even trying. Ask anyone who has ever been through an exercise in reconsidering our constitutional makeup. Ask anyone who, in the Trudeau years, was involved in the repatriation of the Constitution, or in the Meech Lake and Charlottetown agreements of the Mulroney years, or in the Quebec separation referenda. Or ask anyone who has been involved in anything on a national level, whether a national trade association, sporting body, or charity. Doing anything "national" in Canada involves heavy lifting. So, going to the heart of the matter and trying to rearrange the way the country operates is advisedly a fool's errand.

There are many people who have been through these previous adventures. They are members of Canada's "fed-prov" industry, and for the most part, they've convinced themselves not only that nothing can change, but that nothing should change. Many of them are either civil servants or political advisors, and many are journalists. And there is a smattering of constitutional lawyers who have laboured long, and profitably, on these files. They can explain what didn't work, why it didn't work, and why it won't work. Their advice is to work around the stasis, accommodate the dysfunction, limit expectations, and be glad that we seem to be doing okay the way things are.

So when someone like Toronto mayor David Miller talks about something simple like having Ottawa devote one-sixth of its 6 percent

Goods and Services Tax to the cities, the fed-prov boys roll their eyes and say, "Where has he been for the last two decades?" They wonder, often in back rooms and periodically in the op-ed pages of the papers, why he is tilting at windmills.

It is not only the doubters who are wearied from too many battles. The way ahead is also blocked by the entrenched interests of the federal and provincial governments, who have become entirely used to the hearty revenues they can call forth from the big cities—taxes from the businesses and workers who thrive there. Those cities, and the large capital pools that accumulate and operate in them, are an ample and growing supplier to government coffers. There is nothing more appealing to a politician than having access to money that he can award throughout the land, to the plaudits of a grateful citizenry who have quite forgotten that it was their money in the first place. And there is the traditional reluctance of Canadian mayors to raise much of a fuss over these issues, afraid—not without justification—that it might cause them to lose their place at the trough when they are seeking assistance for their city.

So, anyone wanting to design even a little addition to the structure of our country, let alone be the architect of a whole new design, has to take into account a lot of history and a lot of common practice in the federal arts. The country, over all these decades, has not changed so much.

But one thing has changed dramatically, and that is the size and importance of the cities that are now the virtually invisible political entity. They are the missing government in the Canadian polity. But they aren't missing or invisible in their financial, social, and cultural clout. Cities, and the three big-city regions of Vancouver, Montreal, and Toronto in particular, are the major engines of national prosperity and vitality. Canada pays a high price for a political system so comprehensively out of touch with its major assets, so resolutely in thrall to an organizational structure a century out of date.

So it is time to embark on that fool's errand, to begin considering a new Canada that can respond to its current realities and challenges. And, as this book has argued, those centre around the large urban regions, and on the next tier of big cities.

■■■

If you were to sit down with a group of clear-sighted people and design a country for the twenty-first century, what might it look like? Would it have provinces at all? Would it have city-states? If so, what might qualify one place as a city-state over another? What would be the relative roles of the federal, provincial, and municipal governments? Would there be massive municipal amalgamations, with large regional governments? Importantly, what effect would there be on the democratic access of citizens to their governments? These are some of the vast number of questions to be asked.

But any good piece of architecture should start with some design principles. In the case of Canada, they should take the best of what we have, and what we like about our country, and if possible make them better. These are some of the principles that should guide any reconstruction of Canada.

- **Make Democracy Work.** The democratic access of citizens to their governments should be retained and enhanced. Canadians are tired of electing what journalist Jeffrey Simpson has called "benevolent dictators," politicians who consult with us once every four years or so in an attempt to get our vote, then proceed to rule without reference to anything other than public-opinion polls. The increasing centralization of government in the offices of the prime minister or premier in an effort to control all actions and messages is an unfortunate development of recent decades. The new technology of electoral politics has resulted in an ever-finer parsing of the citizenry, with narrow and highly targeted policies and initiatives being aimed at the swing cohorts. Control is everything, and any errant messages or actions are not to be tolerated, so elected members are expected to toe the line drawn by the office of the prime minister or premier. It is not just citizens who are being excluded. Backbenchers, Opposition politicians, and even junior cabinet ministers often have to read the morning newspaper to find out what the government of the day is doing. New governments should take the best practices from the way cities operate, as well as the best federal and provincial practices, to make sure that citizens have a high level of access to governments and many opportunities to make their views heard. There are a number of ways to reopen our politics to citizens. One is by limiting confidence votes in the parliaments, so that a government would not necessarily fall on any vote it lost. This would allow a loosening of party discipline so that individual members might vote on issues either as they thought fit or as they thought their constituents would want. It would allow a broader debate of public issues both in Parliament and its committees. It might also allow some members to become specialists or experts in areas, as Liberal backbencher John Godfrey did on children's issues before he joined the national cabinet. Such an opening up might allow for more robust welcoming of citizen participation in a way that might actually have an impact on the content of the legislation.

- **Understand That Size Matters.** Any public policy that tries to find one size to fit all is doomed. Size increases complexity, and greater

complexity often calls for more complex solutions. And any public policy that tries to find one size to fit all urban areas is equally
doomed. The three large urban regions need extensive revenue
tools, powers, and control over their governance structure—
essentially, the powers of a province in the Canadian context. The
next tier of cities needs much more control of their destinies than
they presently have. A new architecture for Canada has to be willing to countenance such difference in treatment and capacity of
different-sized places.

- **Keep Sharing the Wealth.** The Canadian practice of sharing the wealth
  created in one part of the country with less wealthy areas should
  be continued in some form. There are many criticisms of these
  programs, primarily that they take away initiative and independence of the regions. Critics of the effect of the programs in the
  Maritimes, principally Brian Lee Crowley of the Atlantic Institute
  of Market Studies (AIMS), say they have created regions of
  dependents and shifted decision-making power out of the region
  to the federal government. However, one of the great fears of
  empowering the cities is that the flow of capital to weaker regions
  will be stopped. At least until the country is prepared to evaluate
  and change the transfer system, wealth-sharing programs should
  be maintained so that the empowerment of the city-regions can't
  be characterized as a cash grab.

- **Make Sure the Right Government Does the Right Job.** Subsidiarity is the principle
  that as much as effectively possible should be done at the level
  closest to the citizens being affected, and that central authorities
  should only do those things they can do more effectively. Powers
  should either flow up to the national government (particularly

the setting of standards and the protection of rights) or down to local governments, where power and accountability should rest at the same level. Subsidiarity was a design principle in the creation of the European Union. Some things that are complicated, like welfare, can probably be best administered at a local level, but should be managed financially at the highest level in order to gain the benefits of the resilience of bigger budgets. In financial down- turns, when welfare is most used, the federal government has the greatest capacity to absorb the fiscal stress that might hobble local governments, particularly in smaller centres. This desire to balance local versus central, and to keep authority and account- ability together, is the great design challenge involved in building a new Canada.

- **Balance Representation by Balancing Populations.** The present population imbalance between regions and between provinces is a source of conflict, and could be ameliorated by having units closer in size. At a meeting of Canada's premiers, are they all truly equal, when the Ontario premier represents 100 times as many people as PEI's premier?

■ ■ ■

Let's start with population. The point has been made earlier in this book, but it bears repeating: Prince Edward Island is smaller than twenty-seven cities in Canada, yet it enjoys immensely more power than any of them, or than all of them put together. The Montreal region has twenty-five times the population of PEI, Vancouver fifteen times. But it is easy to pick on PEI, which enjoys both its provincial status and its relatively hefty representation in Parliament because of history. PEI is such an immensely agreeable place that we should not begrudge it. It is just the attractive poster child for the historical anomaly we inhabit.

But a graph of provincial populations represents a steep ski-jump image, with Ontario (close to 13 million) at one end, starting a steep slope to Quebec (7.5 million), BC (4 million), and Alberta (3 million), then levelling off at the rest around a million or less. The territories in the north barely register on the floor of the graph. There is a huge variation, and it can probably never be completely eliminated.

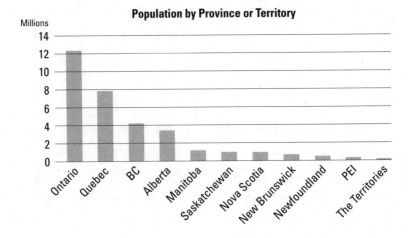

Population by Province or Territory

Why does some equality of population matter? Partly because it will help mitigate the sense that some premiers carry more weight than others. And partly because regions that operate more integrally can focus on supporting and sustaining economic growth and cultural vitality. They can, for example, have more substantive programs to attract and retain immigrants to help build the local economy. They can, at a minimum, eliminate some of the interprovincial trade barriers that have plagued Canada for decades, and which seem harder to eliminate than international barriers.

A New Map of Canada

On a purely population-based approach, two dramatic steps could be taken that would unify two regions and create city-provinces of the three major urban regions. The Maritime Union would unite Nova Scotia, New Brunswick, Prince Edward Island, and Newfoundland; the Prairie Union would unite Manitoba, Saskatchewan, and Alberta; and creating city-provinces would take Vancouver out of British Columbia, Toronto out of Ontario, and Montreal out of Quebec. The populations of the new entities would be a much less steep ski jump.

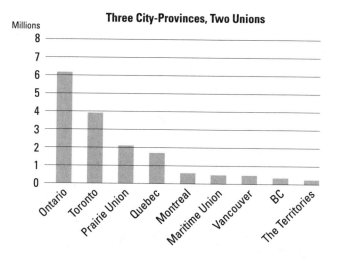

Thus there would be eight provinces and three territories. There would still be imbalances, with the premier of Ontario having three and a half times the constituents of the premier of British Columbia. But generally this configuration achieves as much population equality as possible. It also pays some recognition to regional affinity, at least as understood by a schoolboy growing up in Vancouver in the 1950s with primers full of Prairie wheat and cattle farms and Maritime fish boats and wharves.

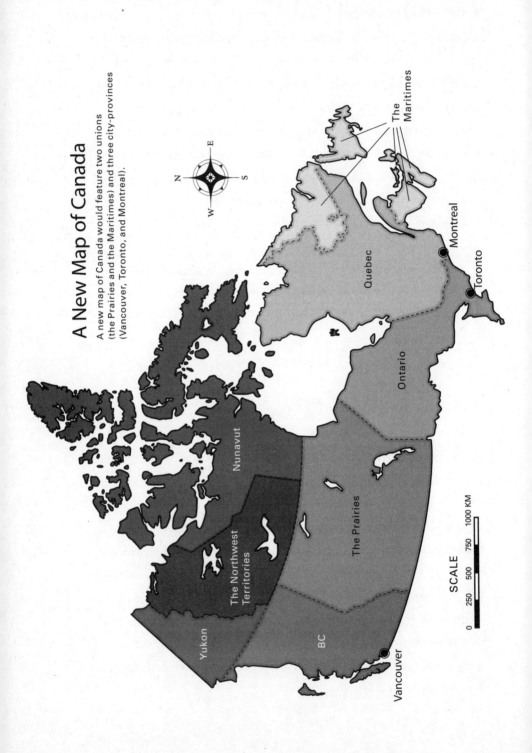

A New Map of Canada

A new map of Canada would feature two unions (the Prairies and the Maritimes) and three city-provinces (Vancouver, Toronto, and Montreal).

The Maritimes

Quebec

Ontario

Montreal

Toronto

Nunavut

The Northwest Territories

Yukon

The Prairies

BC

Vancouver

SCALE

0   250   500   750   1000 KM

N E S W

Other than the normal preference for the known over the unknown, there are a number of holes for such a proposal to fall into. It is hard to know where to start in pointing them out. Tampering with anything in Quebec is hardly a recipe for success. Pulling Montreal out of the province would have implications because it is the least separatist region of the province, and the fastest growing, so the rest of the province would be left as a simmering separatist rump, minus the golden goose. No Quebec government would willingly see the province divided, for fear of losing its bargaining force within Confederation, not to mention its financial engine.

If any part of Canada can rival Quebec for its sense of being unique, it is Newfoundland. There are a good number of Newfoundlanders who believe that joining Canada was a folly perpetrated by the madman Joey Smallwood, and who look at prosperous and independent Iceland as an indication of what might have been. Any attempt to mitigate the strong sense of identity by merging the province with its mainland neighbours, would meet with stout resistance.

As would talk of Maritime Union across the rest of the region. It is not a new conversation. It was a prominent proposal in the years prior to Confederation in 1867, and it led to Nova Scotia and New Brunswick joining Canada. Lieutenant Governor Arthur Hamilton Gordon of New Brunswick had recommended the amalgamation of the three separate colonies of Prince Edward Island, Nova Scotia, and New Brunswick, but the initiative was superseded by Confederation. It has come up again from time to time, with more or less public support, but has foundered on a lack of urgency, bureaucratic indifference to the idea, regional disputes of the day, and a lack of stomach for all the details that would have to be worked out—things like where the capital might be, which program standards might prevail, and how the political parties might meld.

AIMS, which has become an active voice of reform in the region, has an even broader concept than Maritime Union: "Atlantica," which entails a cross-border region encompassing the US New England states. AIMS has developed a considerable argument for Atlantica, a principal component of which is creating direct transportation corridors from the Canadian provinces through Maine, Vermont, and New York into the Montreal and Toronto regions, as well as into New York City. They argue, tellingly, that Atlantica already exists in good part, functionally if not politically. The politicians of the region, Canadian premiers and US governors, meet regularly, and functional cooperation is worked out on a practical basis. As in most things, it is more a matter of deciding how to do something than focusing on why you think it can't be done.

Before European settlement, the Prairie region had various First Nation linguistic groups across it. These, and the tribal distributions, continue to this day. Manitoba joined Confederation in 1870, and Saskatchewan and Alberta followed in 1905. Across their geography, they share much. Farming and ranching have been important activities in all three provinces. In particular, cold-weather farming, and in recent decades large-scale grain farming, have been well developed. Wheat was the undisputed king of the region for the first half of the twentieth century, and Prairie wheat was shipped around the world. Alberta and Saskatchewan both have oil and gas resources that are being vigorously harvested, with Alberta enjoying enormous fortune from it. Saskatchewan has benefited from its great deposits of potash, which it has shipped around the world, and the deposits run across the southern parts of all three provinces.

In recent decades, Alberta has jumped ahead because of its bigger oil deposits, and the province has become an economic powerhouse. The massive oil sands in the north have become viable with the rise in world oil price, making the high production costs of extracting oil from the sand affordable. So prosperous has the northern economy become in places like Fort McMurray that there are labour shortages, requiring fast food companies like Tim Hortons to offer signing bonuses to attract counter employees. Both Calgary and Edmonton have become cities of a million, and the province has gone from being a recipient to a supplier of national subsidies. Some people talk about Calgary and Edmonton as an urban region, but it is a stretch. A stretch of about 250 kilometres, in fact. And along that distance there is much open country. They may act in some ways like joined cities, but they are by no means contiguous.

The population of the three provinces if united would be 5.5 million, of which Alberta would account for 60 percent, and the urban regions of Edmonton, Calgary, Regina, Saskatoon, and Winnipeg would comprise 55 percent. Uniting the Prairie provinces would begin to give the region additional clout and provide some immediate relief from interprovincial trade barriers. Alberta would have serious questions about whether it was "averaging down" its power within Confederation, but the strength of its population within the new Prairie Union, combined with the dominant character of its two main cities, would ensure its continuing prominence.

That prominence, in fact, is one of the best arguments for Prairie Union, because it could be lent to a part of Canada that is less prosperous than Alberta, and which could benefit from both the economic and urban vitality of that province. Neither Saskatchewan nor Manitoba are economic basket cases, having stable long-term resource-based industries like potash, oil and gas, farming, and ranching. But neither have the runaway prosperity of Alberta. And while Winnipeg, with a population of 700,000, is only 30 percent smaller than either Edmonton or Calgary, Regina and Saskatoon—at about 200,000—are fully 80 percent smaller. They are small cities with significant issues, particularly related to strategies for including the Aboriginal communities in the future of the region. Being a part of a larger, more prosperous, and more cooperative union would offer resources and ideas to the whole region.

Whether it was Laurier and Sifton over a century ago, or former Winnipeg mayor Glen Murray talking with Jane Jacobs a decade ago, the relative lack of prosperity from the western edge of the Great Lakes to Calgary is a matter of national concern, and one that calls for dramatic strategies. Prairie Union is one such strategy that may be achievable, given the fact that there is so much shared history, activity, and culture across the region. In fact, it could be well argued that there is much more that unites them than divides them.

Fair Representation in the House of Commons

With Maritime and Prairie unions come the opportunity and requirement to change the distribution of seats in the national House of Commons. The original Confederation, and subsequent adjustments, carried "deal points." There was the so-called "senate floor" provision, and the "grandfather" provision. The first said that no province would have fewer seats in the House than it had in the Senate, so PEI gets four Commons seats rather than the one that its population would warrant. As a result of the grandfather agreement, no province would fall below the number of seats it had at any specific time of readjustment, the last being in 1986, so Quebec has a guarantee of at least seventy-five seats, no matter what its population might warrant. This provision guarantees that provinces declining absolutely in population, or in their percentage share of the population, would not lose seats. This is clearly a bias against fast-growing areas, such as the big-city regions, although it is designed and defended by the courts as a protection of lagging regions. There is also a provision in the Confederation Act of 1867 that allows for the populations of ridings to vary from the national average by 25 percent either way. Given that there is roughly one seat for every 100,000 Canadians, ridings can range from 75,000 to 125,000 residents—meaning the smallest possible riding would be only 60 percent as populous as the largest.

In a new Canada of eight provinces, the initial seat distribution in the House of Commons might be: Ontario, 70; Toronto, 60; Prairies, 55; Quebec, 40; Montreal, 35; Maritimes, 23; Vancouver, 22; BC, 21; Yukon, 1; North West Territories, 1; Nunavut, 1. The House of Commons would have 329 members, an increase over the current 306. The average riding would contain 100,000 people, as it currently does, but discrepancies would be eliminated under this system, making citizens' votes more equal across the country. No longer would a voter in Vancouver cast a vote with less weight than one in the Maritimes. This system would avoid the tremendous disparity of a proposal made in 2007 by the Harper government that by 2014 would see Ontario with 40 percent of the national population and just 35 percent of the Commons seats. Being able to clean up old commitments made over a century ago, but which inhibit the ability of the country to be internationally competitive in the twenty-first century, let alone act with fairness to all its citizens, is a tremendous opportunity for the new Architects of Confederation.

A New Canada

I suggest, then, a set of four steps that can bring a new coherence to politics in Canada, which can come much closer to reflecting the interests and aspirations of citizens. They grow out of a conviction that place matters. And they suppose that a group of citizens, our Architects of Confederation, faced with Canada today, would want to organize the country in a very different way. The four steps:

- Create new city-provinces of Vancouver, Toronto, and Montreal.
- Combine Alberta, Saskatchewan, and Manitoba into one province, the Prairies.
- Combine Newfoundland, Nova Scotia, New Brunswick, and Prince Edward Island into one province, the Maritimes.
- Create 329 federal ridings of equal size, each representing 100,000 people.

Liberated Cities

The greatest benefit of the new arrangements is the liberation of the great urban regions of Canada. The new provinces of Vancouver, Toronto, and Montreal will have been granted control of destiny, which would allow them to build on their strengths in a focused and ambitious way. Vancouver would have the tools to become the undisputed leader of the Cascadia region, the temperate rainforest region that runs from the central coast of California to Alaska. And it would be able to be more aggressive in its long-considered ambition to be the gateway to the Pacific Rim. Long a magnet to Canadians seeking better, although not drier, weather in a big-city context, and recently a magnet for Asian and European investors, drawn by its many qualities, who are buying up the downtown condo towers, Vancouver would be poised to take on a world-city role.

Montreal used to be Canada's biggest city, its financial capital, and the place where all serious things began. It has decisively lost that standing over the last thirty years, and will likely never get it back. But by being separated from the province of Quebec, Montreal could once again assert its cosmopolitan, world-city ways, and begin to regain its old importance commercially, socially, and culturally.

And Toronto could begin to focus on its strengths and channel investment into economic development, including the robust development of research and development, financial services, design and information, and culture, and the remediation of its social issues through the building of affordable and assisted housing. It could also follow the examples of Halifax, Montreal, Quebec City, and Vancouver by recreating its waterfront as a vibrant city neighbourhood.

Through the lens of the key factors of renewal, powers, governance, and finance, the new Canada would have a greater degree of clarity. For most parts of the country, except for the new city-provinces, the powers would remain the same, essentially those of the provinces they were and have become anew. For the new city-provinces of Vancouver, Toronto, and Montreal, there would be a whole new array of powers that would give them greater control of their destinies. In particular, they would have full power over their health and education systems, the two biggest provincial responsibilities in the Canadian context. Importantly, in having these powers, there would be no more excuses, because Canadian provinces have nearly absolute ability to govern in what may be the most decentralized country in the world.

It is in governance and fiscal arrangements that the greatest adjustments would need to be made. In every province, new legislatures would be created. New capitals would have to be designated for the Prairies, Ontario, and the Maritimes, presuming that Quebec City would remain the capital of Quebec, Victoria of BC, and Toronto's Queen's Park would be the Toronto provincial capital. Would Montreal and Vancouver's city halls become the new provincial legislatures? Would one of the old capitals of Edmonton, Regina, or Winnipeg serve the Prairies? Would St. John's, Fredericton, Charlottetown, or Halifax serve the Maritimes? Or might Calgary or Saskatoon, Saint John or Moncton, step forth?

And the political dynamics of the new provinces would have to be worked out. Electoral commissions would have to be established to create, say, the sixty seats of the Province of Toronto, complete with boundaries that would respect the terms of the old Confederation Act on the subjects of geography, history, and identity, all of which are vaguely defined. Once those were worked out, and the real work of governing was begun, how would the politics organize themselves? Which political parties of our current and historic experience would be active, and where? Would the Conservative Party, for example, be an active player in Montreal? While that party has won few seats in recent years in inner-city ridings in Toronto and Vancouver, perhaps under the new regional setups, which would include the outer suburbs, they might find new life, and new policies as they began to appeal to urban voters. Would the Liberal Party, shut out of much of rural Canada, remain shut out? Would the Bloc Québécois dominate Quebec, or would a new party arise to threaten its success there and reduce it to a rump in the federal House?

More importantly, would the issues that dominate the business of the country differ dramatically from what has been the case in our history? A third of the seats would come from the urban provinces, and if you add the Edmonton/Calgary clout of the Prairies, almost half of the voices in the House would be urban-based. There would certainly be more talk of urban transit policy, affordable and assisted housing programs, immigrant settlement policy and programs, and investment incentive programs.

The Difficult Process of Change

But it would take time for the politics to settle down. A look at the city amalgamations that took place in various parts of Canada in the last decades of the twentieth century tell the tale. You can change the form, but the function lags behind as people test out how it works. Otto von Bismarck defined politics as "the art of the possible" (interestingly, in 1867, the year of Canadian Confederation), and it takes time to find out all the things that are possible. But Canadians familiar with Quebec separatism or periods of minority government, are used to unsettled politics. Settle down they usually do, abetted in good times by the presence of strong leaders.

Fiscally, there would have to be many adjustments as new regions worked out new budgets. Again, the municipal amalgamations are instructive. One of the stated reasons for many of the municipal rearrangements was to save money. If you make one fire department out of five, the argument used to go, you'll save money. In fact, what happened was that they always cost more. Five fire chiefs didn't become one fire chief; they became five deputy chiefs and one new chief. Wage rates didn't find a happy medium, but rose to the highest level among the component forces, because of union contract protections that could not be dismantled or negotiated away. There may be reasons for amalgamations, say experts such as Andrew Sancton of the University of Western Ontario or Enid Slack of the University of Toronto, but saving money isn't one of them.

New budgets must be written, new departments configured, new relationships developed, new accountabilities defined. The good news is that this work doesn't have to be done by neophytes. Canada is blessed at every level of government with some of the most able public servants in the world, and in any new function or organization there will be an ample supply of first-class people to design and operationalize the new entity. Nowhere is this truer than in finance. All of the new provinces would find a ready group of capable finance officials to design revenue and expenditure systems and protocols—for the most part simply modifying what already exists across the country and fitting it into the national tax collection and transfer system.

It is important not to trivialize the logistical problems of such a reorganization of the country. But it is equally important not to stick with the status quo because we are unwilling to undertake reform, because we think it will be too difficult. Canadians have done this before—when we made the country in the first place, and in the many additions and alterations we have made since. Such a set of changes may be difficult, but they are by no means prohibitively so.

The biggest adjustments will be political, both for politicians and citizens. Many politicians like the status quo because it serves them well, or at least well enough. Change means a step into unknown territory. They would rather live with the devil they know than the one they don't. And there can be no doubt that some of them would be worse off under such a reformed Canada. Change may well bring forward new leaders, a new cohort of politicians who think and act differently, who want to pursue other issues and agendas, and who have little patience with old ways of doing politics. There may be an influx of formerly municipal politicians from Vancouver, Montreal, and Toronto who demand more openness in government, looser party discipline, and greater citizen engagement in the processes of deliberation. They might be younger, more diverse in terms of both race and gender, like the urban populations from which they come.

Which may unsettle some citizens, too, who have grown used to, even affectionate towards, some of the devils they know. Polls tell us that there is a division between rural and urban Canadians in values, and such a shift in the national consensus towards the larger urban population might leave some rural Canadians feeling as if their country were being taken away from them. Building effective bridges between urban and rural Canada would indeed become one of the great duties of wise politicians, as Senator Hugh Segal has pointed out.

Segal is one of those wise politicians. At the outset of the twenty-first century he noted the oddity of Canada seeming to be in thrall to its Constitution, rather than the Constitution being in service to the country. He has also been at the forefront of the practice of civil politics, which attempts to bind the country in a spirited pursuit of the future rather than a divisive exploitation of its past.

Politicians of Segal's stripe will be required to take Canada into its new future. Perhaps we will need a Sir John A. Macdonald, a person of extraordinary vision, dedication, durability, intelligence, and magnetism to see the future at the same time as ironing out each bump and calming each shudder. It is a task few could accomplish, but it is a task that must be done.

Canada at the start of the twenty-first century is going into the world hobbled—able, but with a self-imposed restraint. The greatest assets we have to compete in the world, our great city regions, are being constrained by history, politics, and regulation. In order to keep our place in a competitive world, let alone advance, we need to liberate them. We can choose to do so slowly with little effect, to take some dramatic steps that will make a difference but still probably leave us in place, or to find the new Architects of Confederation to make a new Canada for the twenty-first century and beyond. Canadians have always had courage, inventiveness, competence, and resolve. It is now time to know whether we are brave enough to make a new future.

ACKNOWLEDGEMENTS

I attended a symposium some years ago to consider the work of Escott Reid, the former Canadian diplomat and first national secretary of the Canadian Institute of International Affairs. Symposium chair Geoffrey Pearson, also a renowned diplomat, opened the session by asking us to consider why the conference was about Escott Reid and not, say, O. D. Skelton, Norman Robertson, or Clifford Clark, more famous public servants who may have had more impact. Pearson answered his own question by saying it was because Reid wrote books, and therefore we know what he thought. Reid left us his impression of the times, a gift to future generations to help us understand those times better.

Urban Nation is not an academic book but an argument for cities, and thus it is relatively devoid of footnotes or the other paraphernalia of scholarly texts. The argument is mine alone but has benefitted in substance and form from the help of many people.

My good friend Joe Berridge, partner at Urban Strategies, is a leading international urban planner, writer, and thinker. He and I talk constantly about the people, activities, and policies that make cities work. Along the coastal path at St. David's in Wales, or aboard his sailboat on Toronto harbour, or eating oysters at a seaside café on the Île de Ré, we have shared ideas, arguments, and enthusiasms for years, and much from those discussions has informed how I think about cities and their place in the firmament. Berridge should be held blameless for the contents of this book, but it would never have been written without his muse.

The late Joe Breiteneicher played a similar role. Joe was president of The Philanthropic Initiative in Boston, a non-profit consultancy in strategic philanthropy that I chaired for many years. He had also been a real estate development executive and social activist over the years, moving seamlessly between sectors. He was an urban enthusiast and advocate, and we roamed cities together, looking, learning, and talking. Joe died too early in the summer of 2007, and we lost a dedicated lover of cities.

I had the privilege of being a colleague and friend of Jane Jacobs, one of the great minds of the twentieth century. I compare Jane to innovative painters, like Manet or Picasso, who helped us see the world from a new perspective. Jane had strong powers of observation, and conversation with her challenged conventional views and illuminated interconnections and complexities.

Helen Walsh is the publisher of the *Literary Review of Canada* and the executive director of Diaspora Dialogues, which helps immigrant writers develop their craft and find markets for their work in Canada. Helen reviewed my book outline and early work to help me get on track, and was an ongoing encouragement to press on.

Jim Gifford, senior non-fiction editor at HarperCollins, approached me with the idea of writing the book, provided key advice on how to organize it and prepare a proper outline, and guided the revisions after the first draft. Without his intelligent guidance and genial stewardship, the task would still be grinding on.

Vali Bennett is director of administration and my assistant at Avana Capital Corporation and The Maytree Foundation. She took away my scheduling privileges years ago and thus is responsible for finding time for me to do things. She took the news that we had to fit book-writing into the schedule with equanimity, and managed both to find the time and to defend my right to write. Without her superior management skills, the book would be only an aspiration. Much of the content of the book, as outlined in the introduction, derives from my activities at Ideas that Matter (ITM). The organization was founded with Mary Rowe, now a vice-president of the Blue Moon Fund in the United States. Mary is the best facilitator of complex ideas and discussions that I've ever encountered, and her energy and effervescence inspired many of the exceptional ideas and achievements of ITM. Mary's able successor at ITM is Ann Peters, who—with her colleagues Stephanie Saunders and Sarah Gledhill—has been very helpful in recalling details of situations and finding appropriate documents.

My colleague Ratna Omidvar, executive director of The Maytree Foundation, is another individual with whom regular and stimulating conversation over the years has helped shape the ideas in the book. One of Maytree's areas of focus is immigration, and through my work on cities, Ratna has integrated the urban focus into Maytree's vision in a powerful way. It is largely through Maytree that I came to see immigration as a dominant twentieth-century trend that shaped Canada, along with urbanization.

Enid Slack is a leading municipal finance expert, well known internationally. She is the director of the Institute on Municipal Finance and Governance at The Munk Centre for International Studies at the University of Toronto. I have learned an enormous amount about finance, the spine of any government's capacity, from Enid, and as chair of the institute, I occupy an ideal perch for more learning. She made it clear to me that understanding how money functions is critical to understanding how governments function.

There have been a number of people from whom I have learned a lot over the years but who will not agree with many of the points or conclusions of this book. Some of them hold dramatically different views from mine and are much more persuasive than I am. I mention them in gratitude for their willingness to share their ideas over the years. Don Stevenson was a senior public servant federally and in Ontario, has been a fellow at the Canadian Urban Institute, and is one of the wisest and most informed commentators on urban issues. Don has always been enormously generous in sharing his knowledge and experience. John Sewell is a prolific writer, an author of books as well as newspaper columns. A former mayor of Toronto, John is an engaged citizen of the city and the country, and can always be counted on to force debate on important ideas and actions. David Crombie, another former Toronto mayor, has spoken and written on a broad range of urban issues. A past president of the Canadian Urban Institute, he has the remarkable ability to look at the current moment in the context of other places and historical moments in time. Anne Golden, Conference Board of Canada president and CEO, and former head of the Toronto United Way, is one of our esteemed authorities on cities. She has always been generous with her ideas and views. And Ken Greenberg, another leading urban planner, has a unique way of combining realism and vision in a way that clarifies the path ahead.

I am grateful to Ken Alexander, editor of The Walrus, for asking me to write the article that formed the basis for this book. Ken has put his passion and intelligence into creating The Walrus, which has become a key conduit for Canadian discourse on important issues. Ken has also generously encouraged and promoted many authors who have written for The Walrus.

I also want to thank my old friends Michael Adams and Patrick Luciani for advice on how to go about writing a book. As people who have done so, they were quite helpful and offered practical tips. Both have the very good sense to deliver advice in pleasant circumstances, usually over a good meal.

My wife, Judy, known to me as "Louie," is the indispensable element in whatever I do. Without her support, encouragement, and accommodation of my work, nothing much would get done. To her, I express my thanks and love.

And my sons, Sam and Matt, are an immense motivation. They are the main reason I think of doing things that last beyond my lifetime. I want them to know that their dad, like their mother, wants to make a better world.

INDEX

"colonist trains," 51
Colosio, Luis Donaldo, 150, 151
commensality, 7
Confederation Act, 222
Conference Board of Canada, 11
Connell, Martin, 136
construction industry, 17, 34–35, 51
　shortage of skilled labour, 60–61
Contemporary Art Gallery, 180
The Creative Class (Florida), 71–72
Crombie, David, 5, 7–9, 95, 97, 118–19,
　129, 132, 138
Crowley, Brian Lee, 214
cultural amenities, 179–80, 184
cultural diversity
　demands placed on health care system
　　by, 100–105, 191–93
　demands placed on school systems by,
　　99–100, 194–95
　promotion through immigration policy,
　　58–59
　in Toronto, 3–4
Cuomo, Mario, 165

D'Alessandro, Dominic, 64
Danson, Barney, 157
Dark Age Ahead (Jacobs), 12
Davis, Bill, 38–39, 73
de Klerk, Frederik Willem, 154–57
density trading, 179–80
deputy mayors, 134–35
Deutsch, John, 167
Diamond, Jack, 17
Diaspora Dialogues, 58–59, 64–65
Doctoroff, Dan, 134–35
downloading, 70–71, 74–76, 107, 137–38,
　162
Drummond, Don, 12
Duerr, Al, 10

Edmonton, Alberta
　receives share of provincial gas tax, 163
　suburbs, 33
education. *See also* public schools;
　　universities and colleges
　accessibility for immigrants, 177–79, 184
　barriers to immigrants, 61–63
　municipal control over, 71–72
　and training, 37–39
employment
　accessibility for immigrants, 60, 63,
　　105–6
　concentration in cities, 30

entertainment industry, 36–37, 53
environmental policy, 197–98
equalization payments, 2–3, 41, 114, 167,
　214
Europe, immigration to Canada from,
　48–49, 51–54
European Union, charter on cities, 8
Evolution of Toronto conference, 7–9
excise taxes, 110, 117–18
　municipal, 126
Expo 86, 91–93

federal government
　ability to help cities, 168–84
　backlog of immigration cases, 61
　centralization of decision-making,
　　212–13
　decisions driven by political
　　considerations, 101, 105, 113–14,
　　115–16
　downloading of costs on provinces, 74,
　　79, 107
　efficiency relative to municipal
　　governments, 97–98, 114–15, 186
　funding of immigrant settlement, 181
　funding of urban infrastructure, 68–70,
　　73–74
　grants to cities, 80–82, 162–63
　grants to individuals, 169, 176–80, 181
　housing policy, 158, 170, 174
　imposition of "one size fits all" solutions,
　　213–14
　indifference to Toronto, 4, 72, 73
　indifference to urban affairs, 9–12, 14,
　　113–16, 158–59, 182–83
　influence over municipal budgets, 70
　influence over municipal priorities,
　　68–70, 94, 172
　interest in urban affairs, 73, 157–58
　possessiveness towards tax revenue,
　　114, 211
　sources of tax revenue, 110
　transfer of power to provinces, 168
　transportation policy, 170
　view of municipal politicians, 163–64
Federation of Canadian Municipalities, 8,
　9, 169
"fed-prov" industry, 210–11
financial services industry, 17–18
First World War, effect on urbanization,
　32–33
Flaherty, Jim, 69–70, 163
Flisenberg, Gerarda, 51

Flisenberg, Peter, 51
Florida, Richard, 71–72
Four Pillars Drug Strategy, 130, 160
Fox, Vicente, 151
Franks, C.E.S. (Ned), 143, 204
Friedman, Avi, 174
Fulton, Robert, 26

gasoline tax, shared with cities, 160, 162,
    163, 169
Geary, Peter, 54
gentrification, 112, 123, 175
Gerretsen, John, 96
Gertler, Meric, 7–9
Gibbins, Roger, 12
Gilbert, Richard, 69
Gillies, James, 17
Gladwell, Malcolm, 89
glasnost, 153
Godfrey, John, 213
Godsall, Jay, 100–102
Goldberger, Paul, 135
Golden, Anne, 8–9, 11, 161
Golden Ears Bridge, 121
Goods and Services Tax (GST)
    rebates paid to cities, 162–63, 176
    Toronto's campaign to share in, 115–16,
        210–11
Gorbachev, Mikhail, 152–53, 156–57
Gordon, Arthur Hamilton, 219
governance
    cities' control over, 71
    municipal political parties, 138–44
    styles, 131–38, 144–46
Granatstein, Jack, 167
Greater Golden Horseshoe (GGH), 187
Greater Toronto Area. *See* Toronto, Ontario
Greater Vancouver Transportation
    Authority, 121
Greenberg, Ken, 17, 78–79
Grow Home, 174
Guelph, Ontario, 30
gun control, 198
Gwyn, Richard, 7–9

Hall, Barbara, 7–9, 129–30, 161
Hamburg, Germany, 190
Hamilton, Ontario, 29, 30
Harcourt, Mike, 98
Harper, Stephen, 113–14, 157
Harris, Mike, 94
    antagonism towards Toronto, 75–76

cancellation of anti-racism programs,
    99–100, 195
and downloading of costs on cities, 74
Head, Ivan, 10–11
health-care system, unique demands in
    cities, 100–105, 191–93
hepatitis C, 192
Highland Clearances, 47
Hohler, Bob, 90
homelessness, 87–91
housing
    federal policy, 158, 170, 174
    low-income, 130, 158, 173–76, 183–84
    transitional, 105–6
human capital, 37–38
    emphasis on immigration policy, 61
    federal investment, 169–70
    infrastructure, 71–72
human immunodeficiency virus (HIV), 192
Hunter, Laird, 174

Ideas (CBC Radio), 8
Ideas That Matter, 6–7
immigrants. *See also* cultural diversity
    active recruitment of, 47–49
    attraction to largest cities, 3, 15, 16, 30,
        36, 42, 50–55, 105–7, 196–97
    barriers to job market, 60, 63, 105–6
    in colonial era, 45–47
    higher incidence of certain infectious
        diseases, 191–92
    settlement of, 56–58, 60–66, 105–7,
        181–82, 184, 196–97
    transitional housing, 105–6
immigration, 45–66. *See also* cultural
    diversity
    barriers to, 56, 57, 60–62
    catalysts, 47
    humanitarian considerations, 58
    policy, 57–59, 178
    slowdown after First World War, 49
    success stories, 51–58
    trends since Second World War, 49–55
"import replacement," 26
income taxes, 110
    dedicated surcharges, 124
    deductibility of transit passes, 171
    municipal, 12, 126
"incremental" houses, 174
Indo-Canadian Chamber of Commerce,
    57–58
Industrial Revolution, 26–28

industrialization, 26–28, 29, 32–33
infectious disease, 100–103, 191–92
information economy, 51, 52–53
International Centre for Infectious Disease, 101
Ireland, immigration to Canada from, 47

Jacobs, Jane, 26, 161
  Dark Age Ahead, 12
  distaste for public-private partnerships, 122
  distaste for Robert Moses, 135
  at Evolution of Toronto conference, 7–9
  on growth of cities, 27–28
  influence over urban thinking, 5–7
  and "New Deal for Cities," 72
  opposition to Spadina Expressway, 73
  and organization of C5 mayors, 10, 11
Jardin Botanique de Montréal, 130

Kanter, Ron, 94–95
Kennedy, Ian, 18
Kent, Tom, 62, 176, 178
Keynes, John Maynard, 199
Khrushchev, Nikita, 153
Kilbourn, William, 5
Kitchen, Harry, 12, 125
Kolb, Emil, 202
Kuprie, Martin, 54

La Guardia, Fiorello, 135
labour markets
  accessibility for immigrants, 60, 63–64, 105–6
  concentration in cities, 30
Lachine, Quebec, 30
land-use planning, 77–79, 94, 197–98
language barriers, and health care system, 103, 192
Lastman, Mel, 9–10
Laurier, Wilfrid, 47–49
Leacock Society, 54
Lee, Susur, 54–55
London, Ontario, 29
Long Branch, Ontario, 30
Loughborough University, 40–41
Louisbourg, Nova Scotia, 24
low-income housing, 130, 158, 173–76, 183–84

Macdonald, Sir John A., 28–29
Macintosh, Bill, 167

Macquarie North America, 121–22
Mance, Jeanne, 24
Mandela, Nelson, 154–56
Manitoba, 220. *See also* Prairie provinces
  income taxes shared with cities, 163
Maritime provinces
  immigration during colonial era, 46
  Maritime Union, 217, 219–20
  slow growth of, 29–30
Markham, Ontario, 100
Martin, Paul
  and downloading of costs, 74, 79
  interest in urban affairs, 72, 75, 157, 160
Mau, Bruce, 17
Maxwell, Wendy, 18
mayors
  as advocates for cities, 9–12, 72, 211
  under strong-mayor system, 133–36
  under stronger-mayor system, 136–38
  under weak-mayor system, 131–33
Maytree Foundation, 63–64
McCallion, Hazel, 202
McCarney, Patricia, 7–9
McGuinty, Dalton, 84, 94, 201
  and City of Toronto Act, 98
  interest in urban affairs, 161–62, 165
Melville Charitable Trust, 90
Metrolinx, 205–6
Metropolitan Toronto. *See also* Toronto, Ontario
  amalgamation, 9, 75–76, 137, 202
  distinct identities of component cities, 189
Mexico, 150–52
Millennium Scholarship Fund, 169, 177, 184
Miller, David
  election of, 11
  interest in immigrant settlement, 106
  and municipal voting rights for non-citizens, 65
  at odds with Joe Volpe, 94, 160
  One Cent Now campaign, 115–16, 210–11
  plans for Toronto waterfront, 94
Miller Group, 121–22
Mimico, Ontario, 30
Mirvish, David, 7
Mississauga, Ontario, 100, 202
Moist, Paul, 12
Monaco, 190
Montreal, Quebec, 24
  case for provincial powers, 98–100